THE LADY
WHO FOUGHT

*A young woman's account
of the Anglo-Boer War*

BY

SARAH RAAL
(MRS O J SNYMAN)

THE LADY
WHO FOUGHT

A young woman's account
of the Anglo-Boer War

BY

SARAH RAAL
(MRS O J SNYMAN)

Translated from the original Afrikaans
by Karen Smalberger
with an introduction
by Anne Emslie

*This publication is dedicated to the memory
of all the women of South Africa who endured suffering
and hardship during the Anglo-Boer War*

STORMBERG
PUBLISHERS

2000

Distributed in southern Africa by Book Promotions,
P O Box 5 • Plumstead 7800 • South Africa;
and in the United Kingdom by Central Books,
99 Wallis Road • London E9 5LN • England

First published in Afrikaans as *Met Die Boere In Die Veld* by Nasionale Pers Bpk in 1936

ISBN 0-620-25406-8

COVER DESIGNED BY JOY WRENCH
SET BY EILEEN EAGAR
PRINTED AND BOUND IN THE REPUBLIC OF SOUTH AFRICA
BY THE RUSTICA PRESS, NDABENI, WESTERN CAPE

D7902

Contents

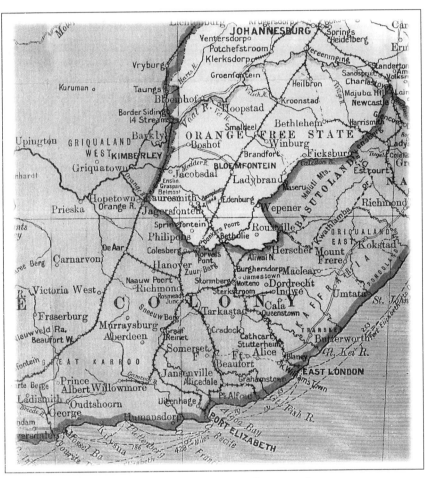

The Orange Free State and surrounds.

Introduction

The story of *The Lady Who Fought* was committed to writing some thirty five years after the experiences it describes. It is a simple, unvarnished tale, told with deep feeling. It retains the flavour and authenticity of oral history, of personal memory, of events told and retold. It is a singular account of the Anglo-Boer War from the unusual perspective of a young woman unwittingly caught up in the sweeping vortex of unfolding action on the veld. As such it is unique.

Sarah Raal is 'the lady who fought' on commando with the Boers, who slept under the open stars, who experienced the continual anxiety of attack, the hardships of weather and the shortage of food. She held her own with the men, bravely insisting on playing her part in ambushes, forays on enemy forces and flight on horseback under fire. To describe her as fearless is inexact. More to the point, her account describes her deep fears, her heartfelt suffering at what she saw and experienced, and her remarkable courage and defiance in the face of hardship and danger.

It is no surprise that Sarah Raal became a heroine among her own people, and notorious among the British forces. At last, when she was taken prisoner, she suffered the indignities attendant upon fame. As a woman who assumed the right to fight like a man for what she held precious, she defied conventional gender roles. She was stared at and whispered about as she travelled under guard from one place of captivity to another. She was mercilessly interrogated, and was subjected to the unspeakable harshness of solitary confinement, which very nearly killed her. Ultimately she retained her self-respect and gained the respect, if at times grudgingly, of even her captors.

'Miss Raal, according to this letter you are the lady who fought,' was the statement put to Sarah by an English officer, Captain Reed, entrusted at one time with her interrogation. Amid the inhuman actions of war, this encounter with the young Boer woman stands out as an episode of nobility, of personal morality and empathy, penetrating the surrounding ruthlessness of war. Sarah Raal movingly describes her initial distrust at encountering Captain Reed's unexpected kindness and courtesy. It is a telling episode in which the general brutality of warfare, by contrast, is shockingly exposed.

In many respects the Anglo-Boer War was a brutal and shocking war. The scorched earth policy adopted by the British led to the detention of women and children in camps, the burning of farmhouses, the ruination of the land, and the wholesale slaughter of animals. 'Had I not seen it myself, I would never have believed that people existed who were capable of such cruelty. But these people would probably have done anything to starve out the Boers,' Sarah Raal comments after witnessing hundreds of sheep left dying in a deliberately torched expanse of grassland. She witnessed, too, the suffering of Boer women and children in the concentration camps, where an estimated 28 000 died, about four times the number of Boer casualties in the field. She saw children, not yet dead, being carried to the morgue, and other unspeakable horrors. She herself was told, 'What is more, you will die here!' by the Commandant of the camp at Springfontein. Instead she escaped.

If Sarah Raal transgressed unquestioned codes of conduct pertaining to the deportment and genteel behaviour of women, the Anglo-Boer War broke many previously held rules of warfare. A new era had broken loose, one in which the British military forces were no longer simply engaging the active fighting force of the Boers, but were in truth waging a war against the entire Boer population. The women, by virtue of their widespread detention, were pulled directly into the arena of the conflict, and an unwritten code was thereby broken. The war was not only a man's war. How apt then that Sarah Raal preferred the battlefield to the constraints and indignities of life in the camps.

The story of Sarah Raal reveals the dark and wantonly destructive heart of a cruel war that left a legacy of death, pain, despair and hatred. And yet there is the marvel of individual courage and sacrifice, of deep love for family and land, of selfless surrender to a cause, of unshakeable loyalties. Sarah Raal embodied such qualities, as did many others caught up in the unstoppable and tragic tide of the war. It was a war that involved the entire country, irrespective of race and creed, although the Boers initially viewed the conflict as a white man's war. The British policy of employing Black men to serve as scouts and spies created division among the Blacks, some of whom allied themselves with the British while others remained fiercely loyal to the Boers. Sarah recounts an incident involving the foreman on her family farm, Andries, who had worked for her father for twenty seven years:

'I was shocked when I was told that Andries had left the farm the previous evening with all his belongings. I then called for Sam, Tryn's husband, who told me that Andries had for some time been talking about defecting to the English. It was said that the English looked after farm workers very well—they were given a rifle and a uniform, and on top of that they were well paid if they joined up.'

The Boers were outraged by the involvement of Blacks in the war by the British. Feelings ran high on this issue, as they did over the 'hensoppers'—Afrikaners who submitted to the British for their own safety and to protect their property—and 'joiners,' who actually defected to and fought for the enemy. Both 'hensoppers' and 'joiners' were viewed by the Boers as traitors, worthy only of scorn and derision, and Sarah Raal's story reflects the nuanced complexities of these divisions, and the intensity of the emotions spawned by them.

Unquestionably the Anglo-Boer War left deep scars on the psyche of the Boer people. The subsequent rise of Afrikaner nationalism has origins in the traumatic events of these years. Sarah Raal's foreword is itself evidence of this. Like the stories of subsequent atrocities in South Africa and elsewhere in the world, we are reminded by the story of Sarah Raal that the past lives on in the present. And indeed that it is fitting to keep alive a sense of outrage at acts of barbarism and betrayal.

How poignant it is to consider Sarah Raal's astonishment that some Afrikaners could act without the slightest concern for what was happening in the camps on their doorstep, together with her remark concerning a German woman who took her in for a night *en route* to the camp at Outdshoorn: 'I wasn't afraid to speak to her openly because I knew what the Germans had done for us in the concentration camps.'

The simplicity of Sarah Raal's account masks the inner sophistication of a young woman devoted to the Boer cause. She was brave in action, but confessed her fear. Under interrogation she was haughtily impertinent and rude, yet privately anxious and afraid. She expressed hatred for the English, yet she wept for an Englishman in distress and acknowledged the friendship of an English officer. She despised the treachery of 'Khaki-Boers,' the 'joiners' and the Black upstarts who threw their weight around on the farm where she was a virtual prisoner, yet she reciprocated the loyal devotion of many Black farm labourers and received steadfast protection from those not intimidated by the occupying forces. Her sadness was relieved by a sense of humour, her despair by her appreciation of nature and acts of human kindness. Overriding all else was her devotion to her parents, her brothers on commando, and the family farm which for her was almost sacred. The harshness of war was forced upon her, a simple Boer girl on her parents' farm, but she rose superior to misfortune and survived to the bitter end, uncompromised and uncompromising.

Throughout the bitterness and struggle of war, Sarah Raal kept her heart intact. She never lost her sense of horror at what she saw and experienced. To maintain a sense of horror in the face of atrocity is an act of humanity. And a heart that does not stop feeling, irrespective of the polarities of warfare, has a rare and impartial strength. The 'lady who fought' is to be much admired for her daring, her courage, her humanity, her heart. Also that she cared enough to tell her story, prodding us not to forget the important lessons of history.

Anne Emslie
January 2000

FOREWORD

Prompted by the requests of many friends, a sense of duty to my people, and to satisfy the wishes of my children, I have recorded here my personal experiences and recollections of the Second War of Independence.

My hope and expectation is that the effort will prove worthwhile, and that it will contribute to an awakening sense of patriotism and nationhood in the younger generation, and strengthen the ties which bind us together as an Afrikaner people.

Sarah Raal
1936

Olijvenfontein, the farm on which Sarah Raal was born
and which to her was 'almost sacred'.

ONE

At the foot of a large ridge covered in olive trees and broom bushes lies Olijvenfontein, my father's beautiful big farm. The farmhouse, a massive old building with a high stoep, thick walls and airy rooms, stands majestically surrounded by green trees. Below it lie the farm lands and a wonderful view over the endless plains of the southern Free State.

Here I first saw the light of day and here we lived quietly and peacefully together as a family until the dark clouds of war gathered over our country, and in 1899 finally brought a violent and inexorable end to the life we'd always known.

I remember as if it were yesterday the troubled feelings of fear and anxiety that grew stronger and stronger as danger approached. Terrifying reports—some true, others not—reached us on a daily basis, creating a mood of uncertainty and apprehension that was evident in my dear mother and father more than anyone else. The happy and carefree atmosphere that had existed in our family circle gave way to a sombre air. So things continued until they came to a head one summer's afternoon in October 1899.

How unforgettable that day was. War was declared and the men called up. Within twenty four hours they were off, with horses, saddles, bridles, and rations sufficient for eight days. The farm was a hive of activity. My dear father, deeply aware of what was happening, and with a profound understanding of the possible consequences, calmly and efficiently gave instructions to his sons and to the farm labourers.

My four brothers were called up first. My father was to follow later. Still young and inexperienced, and with only a vague idea of what it all might mean, they seemed excited, even enthusiastic about what was happening. Saddles and bridles were checked, horses readied; and rifles, cartridges and clothing were put in order.

The farmhouse was no less busy. We had much work to do packing clothes and food for my brothers—*droë wors*, biltong, rusks and other provisions. My mother wandered restlessly from one room to the next, fetching first a pair of socks, then a shirt, then some other item, saying, 'Child, put this in as well, you might need it.' She was unable to talk about the coming war. One minute she would be brave, the next the tears of a worried mother would rise unbidden to her eyes, only to be wiped away with the corner of her old blue apron.

The evening meal passed in uneasy silence. After supper my father said prayers as usual. He prayed earnestly and at length for light and guidance in these dark days. The following day, after all preparations were complete, the horses were saddled, and the hour of parting arrived. One by one we hugged my brothers tightly and wished them well. Tears rolled freely down my mother's face. She could barely manage to say, 'Please be careful, my children.' Apron held to her mouth, she waved them a last goodbye; and watched until they disappeared behind the ridge. Then she took my father's arm and returned to the house, to her bedroom, where she could freely give vent to the anxious thoughts crowding one another in her troubled mind. What would become of them? Would she ever again see her four beloved sons, the youngest of whom was only seventeen?

Three months later my father was also called up. Only my mother, my youngest brother, a little sister and I remained on the farm. Father was not gone long, however—due to his physical condition he returned just three months later.

One morning, about a month after my father's return, we awoke to a perfect summer's day. All of nature seemed serenely at peace, birds were singing in the trees, and a fresh breeze carried the sweet smell of flowers and herbs over the ripe yellow wheat fields. There was no hint of the destruction and bloodshed going on throughout the country. The peace and quiet were, however, of short duration. By late afternoon, a large contingent of English troops arrived on our farm and announced their intention to camp overnight. First the scouts went through everything, then the troops arrived, and the peaceful silence of the day was shattered by upheaval and confusion. Their horses, mules, oxen and other animals were chased into our wheat fields, to eat and trample to their heart's delight, and the men took complete control of the house, so that by the following morning it was utterly devastated.

It rained during the night, and the next day the wheat fields resembled a mud bath. The animals and the rain had so transformed the fields that there was hardly an ear of wheat left standing. The yard and the house were plundered. The soldiers slaughtered and took almost all the poultry, not even female turkeys sitting on their eggs were spared, and cutlery and other household goods were seized. I caught one soldier in the act of hiding knives and spoons in his puttees. He was quick to flee as soon as he saw me.

My father was called to account for his movements during the previous months—where he had fought, where the Boers were, and whether any of his sons were still fighting. When they heard he had four sons on commando, the officer said, 'So, they're fighting while you take care of the farm. Well then, let's take you with us right away.' Before we knew what was happening, and without my father being allowed back into his own house, nor to

9

bid us a proper farewell, we watched him being led away by the officers. With his head lowered, hat in hand, and his bald head in the sun, he turned to us and called, 'Till we meet again!'

Whatever my mother was thinking, it was clear she hadn't grasped what was happening. Only after the troops had left, and I had explained things to her, did she realise that her husband had been taken captive, and was probably on his way to a concentration camp. The same troops that took my father also took all our flour and groceries, as we were accused of giving supplies to the Boers. We then got a pass which enabled us to go to Jagersfontein station, twenty four miles away, every fortnight, to collect the next fortnight's supply of food. They could not starve us out, however. We were still the fortunate owners of forty sacks of wheat and two thousand head of small livestock.

Despite the troubles that beset us, a period of relative monotony followed. Very few people were about. There were only women on the neighbouring farms. The young men were on commando and the older ones had been sent to camps, which left the women in charge of farming operations. In the absence of their bosses, the farm labourers became so difficult and belligerent that we could do nothing with them. If things went even slightly wrong, they refused to work or threatened to report us to the English. As a result farming slowly deteriorated. Signs of decay were clearly visible, bringing on a mood of distraction and despondency.

My mother, who was getting on in years, had lost her former courage. She grieved the days and the weeks away. There was no news. Occasionally we would hear reports of the boys, sometimes disturbing, sometimes reassuring. Thus things continued in uncertainty and anxiety. We hardly ever saw a newspaper, and when we did the news was usually untrue and misleading. Nobody could ride on horseback without the English making inquiries, so we were virtually prisoners on our own farm.

The time came for us to collect provisions again. We always tried to get as much as we could so we would have something to give the burghers if they arrived. They had to be extremely careful as our farm was very close to Kruger station, and it was only under cover of darkness that they could visit us with any degree of safety.

About three months after my father was taken captive, a large Boer commando arrived on the farm, intending to press on that same night. We'd been warned by the English that we'd be in trouble if we didn't inform them of the presence of any Boer commando on the farm, but we would never have considered doing such a thing. The farm workers were used to burghers arriving from time to time—one of them, Andries, had worked for my father for twenty seven years.

Three days after the commando's visit we had to collect a fresh supply of food from Jagersfontein. Because the pass was in my mother's name, she went to collect the provisions accompanied by my younger brother and sister, and I stayed behind on the farm alone. They were due back in the afternoon and I had lots of work to do.

During the afternoon, about the time they were due back, I took the binoculars and went to sit on the ridge behind the house to watch the road. Afternoon turned to early evening, but there was no sign of them. I started to worry. To ease my mind, I told myself there'd probably been some delay, and that they'd be back at any moment. At length it grew dark. There was still no sign of them. I could no longer see the road, so I decided to return to the house. By now I'd given up all hope of their arrival. I called for Tryn to come and sleep in the house with me; and also for Andries, to ask him what I should do, and to find out if there was still a horse available so I could send a youngster from the farm to find out what had happened.

I was shocked when I was told that Andries had left the farm the previous evening with all his belongings. I then called for Sam, Tryn's husband, who told me that Andries had been talking for some time about defecting to the English. It was said that the English looked after farm labourers very well—they were given a rifle and a uniform, and on top of that they were well paid if they joined up. Suddenly things began to make sense—I realised why Andries had become so difficult lately, and why there'd been a light burning in his hut until late the previous night.

Now a new fear took hold of me, and many alarming thoughts flashed through my confused mind. Outside it was dark and ghostly. Inside the large house, all appeared even quieter and darker. Here I was, a young woman just into my twenties, vulnerable and alone, with only the farm labourers for company. Every creek of a floor board or flapping of bats' wings sent cold shivers down my spine. I imagined any number of ghostly figures watching me from every dark nook and cranny of the house. Feelings of anxiety and despair filled me with panic, and I had an overwhelming desire to run from the house. But outside it was equally dark and terrifying, and who knew what danger might await me there ... Andries!

It was now about ten o'clock and Tryn, who had quickly gone to attend to her little ones, returned. I hadn't yet eaten and didn't feel hungry. We made sleeping arrangements. Sleep—who could sleep under such circumstances? I shuddered at the thought of sleeping alone in a dark room. That night I was afraid of the house, afraid of everything. Eventually Tryn convinced me to go to bed. 'Tomorrow they'll come back, *kleinmies*, then everything will be all right,' were her words of comfort.

But I could not sleep. I tossed and turned, devising any number of strategies to deal with my predicament. I was so confused I had no idea what to do. Every time I came up with a solution, some nightmare thought would banish the faint hope I'd managed to kindle. Then I would start all over again. Suddenly

Andries came to mind with such clarity that I sat bolt upright. I was scared of him ... where was he? Would he not come and attack me? In my mind's eye I imagined him creeping towards my window. I was so terrified that I almost cried out, but the loud snoring of Tryn sleeping peacefully in the next room set my mind slightly at ease and made me feel somewhat safer. My mind was again assailed by a multitude of thoughts.

I went over what had happened. The mysterious disappearance of my mother, Andries' stories and then departure—I was beginning to get the gist of it. Connecting the two events, I felt sure I had the solution. It was clear. Andries had informed the English of the visit from the Boer commando, and as a result my mother had been taken captive at the station. This thought destroyed my last faint hope that they would return. Again I sat up in bed, and this time lit the lamp. What would happen to me here alone on the farm? Would they come and take me as well, set fire to our house, and destroy all my father's work? My poor mother would not be able to endure so many shocks one after the other—sent away without money or clothes or anything, and to who knew where, perhaps not even the same camp as my father. Parted from her husband, her four sons at war, perhaps dead by now, and I—her daughter—all alone on the farm! I lay awake mulling things over until dawn. Then I got up and, with the light of a new day, began to gather some courage and hope. Tryn made breakfast, as by that stage I had a headache from lying awake all night on an empty stomach, and I again took the binoculars and returned to the ridge to watch the road.

I paid no attention to the farm—Sam would have to keep everything in order. My only thought was for my own safety and for that of my mother. The idea that she might have been taken captive weighed heavily on me, but I continued to nurture the slender hope that she would return, and kept scanning the road. Afternoon came. Still there was no sign of a cart. After lunch I returned to the ridge with the binoculars. I also made plans to send one of the young farm hands to look for my mother, but this was forbidden and could cause more trouble. It was getting late. The rocks were now casting long shadows. My eyes were sore from watching the distant road, which was now fading with the dusk. There was no sign of life whatsoever.

As day turned to night, hope gave way to shadowy feelings of despondency and despair. I'd received no word or tiding by evening on the second day! There was nothing to be done but return to the big, empty house, for which I now felt a strange fear. I collapsed into a large chair, mentally and physically exhausted. Tryn found me there and tried as best she could to comfort me and give me courage. Finally she coaxed me to bed and made a cup of tea. After again lying awake mulling over my problems, sleep eventually claimed me. Overcome by tiredness, I managed to sleep reasonably well. Next morning I was up early, but by now I'd given up all hope of my mother's return. Instead I tried to concentrate on my own problems, but I was so light-headed and my thoughts were so muddled that I couldn't think straight. There was also no one for me to talk to.

There I was with a whole farm to run, more than two thousand sheep, horses and cattle, and lots of equipment. What was I to do with it all? In my father's trunk in the house was £500 along with all his papers. What were my options? Should I seek enemy protection and shelter while my parents were in a concentration camp, and my brothers on commando? Never! I would rather flee or join a commando myself. I couldn't abandon everything to the enemy without doing my best to accomplish something, but what could I do? Maybe the enemy would come for me, and take everything anyway. I had to secure the money and other things, but how? I started planning to flee, but couldn't fathom how or where to go. First, I decided to take care of the money. What would be safest? To bury it? No, the notes would get wet and disintegrate. After much deliberation I decided to keep the money on me. Eighteen pounds were in gold, and this I worked into a linen band which I tied around my hat and covered with a black band. The rest, about £500 in notes, I sewed into the hem of one of my dresses, and kept just £6 in my purse. If I wore the dress and kept my hat on, I could keep all the money on me.

Now that the money was safe, I felt more at ease—ready to flee if necessary. It was three days since my mother and the others' disappearance, and still there was no news. Who knew, maybe the English would come for me too. There was nothing to be done but wait for events to unfold. I wandered listlessly from room to room, at the same time trying to mask my fear, for Sam and Tryn might get jittery, and what would happen to me if they decided to leave? The days and nights were long and lonely, and I began to wish that something—anything—would happen, just to relieve the monotony. Nothing did. A week went slowly by.

Then, one morning early, an anxious Tryn came to my room, '*Kleinnooi*, quick, you must get up, horsemen are approaching. It looks like the English.'

In a flash I was out of bed, slipped on the dress with the money in it, put the hat on my head, locked the house, and stood waiting on the stoep.

No sooner had I done so than African scouts arrived and approached me in a hostile and belligerent manner. 'We know you give food and money to the Boers,' they said. 'Now we're going to show you a thing or two.'

Then the enemy arrived, wanting to enter the house, but of course they found all the doors locked. An officer approached me saying, 'Well, Miss Raal, have you heard from your mother?'

'No, I have not!' I replied. 'Do you have news of her?'

'Yes, she's been taken captive and sent away.'

'Why was she taken?'

'A Boer commando came past here, and you didn't tell us. It

won't help to discuss it now. We've come to collect money. Your foreman, Andries, told us about the food and money you give to the Boers.'

'Well, there's the house, go and take the money.'

A few of them entered the house and began their search. After a while a soldier found my clothes cupboard, and came across the purse with a few pounds in it.

'Where is the rest?' the officer asked.

'That you must ask Andries,' I replied.

He threw down the purse, and as he left he warned me to be very careful. They would imprison me if I gave the Boers food or anything else—even if the Boers merely came on to the farm. He told me they would be keeping an eye on me from the station, and that from now on they would send Andries daily to check up on me. With that they left. Thank the Lord, the money was still safe.

I now knew that my mother and the others had been taken captive and sent to a camp, but I had no idea where. I still had no news of my dear father, or of my brothers, and I tried to focus instead on the challenges facing me. If only I could remain on the farm undisturbed I would survive; but the station was close by, and I received regular visits from armed African scouts. Some of Andries' children, who wanted nothing to do with him, remained on the farm, and they always warned me when he was coming.

Months went by, months filled with anxiety, worry and stressful uncertainty. I'd had no word of any of my family, and I felt vulnerable and exposed to many kinds of danger. I was, however, determined to stick it out to the bitter end. Every now and then I heard disturbing reports of suffering and death in the camps, and the idea that I could still be taken captive and sent to a camp prompted me to make preparations to flee should it become necessary. Seven months passed in this way, until one morning Tryn came into my room and said, '*Kleinnooi, kleinnooi*, come and look who's here—the *kleinbasies*!'

Imagine my delight and excitement! With tears running down my cheeks, I embraced my brothers, one after the other. The poor boys, will I ever forget the sight of them that day? Tanned, emaciated, weather-beaten, neglected, their shoes almost worn to bits, their clothing all tattered and in shreds. They were excited to be back home, but instead of a hearty welcome they found only an empty house and a helpless sister.

When I was able to speak, I asked, 'Have you come to fetch me?'

They looked at each other quizzically, then said, '*Ag*, sister, how can we take you with us? Our own lives are continually in danger and full of upheaval. We can't stay here either; it's too close to the enemy, and if they knew we were here your life would also be in danger.'

We spent the day very quietly. Their horses were well fed in the stable; and we kept watch for African scouts, for I knew that if they discovered my brothers on the farm it would be the end of me. Late that afternoon I heard from one of Andries' sons that his father knew about my brothers, and that he would be coming with the English that night to capture them. We watched the roads vigilantly and at dusk my brothers saddled up, put me on a horse, and we left together for Toomfontein, a neighbouring farm about half an hour's ride away. We spent the night there, and the following morning my brothers left to rejoin their commando. Then Sam arrived with news of the farm, and told me what had happened the previous night after our departure. The English had arrived with Andries, all armed and on horseback. After hiding their horses, they had surrounded the house in order to capture the Boers they thought were there. When none materialised, they wanted to know from Sam where the Boers were. But Sam said he knew nothing of any Boers, that there were no Boers there, and that my brothers weren't there either. At first light they went into the house and searched it from kitchen to attic. Then they wanted to know what had happened to the girl who lived there. Finding nothing and nobody, and having been told that I'd gone visiting and would be back later that day, they left the farm.

That afternoon I returned home and found everything peaceful and quiet. However, the reports of my brothers' visit had made the English more suspicious than ever. They didn't trust the quiet and, as they desperately wanted to capture my brothers, they did all they could to ensure that if my brothers did return to the farm they would certainly be captured. Every night they sent out African scouts under the leadership of Andries. He knew the farm like the back of his hand, and told them where to hide their horses, and which route my brothers were likely to take to the farm. He also knew the house inside out, including which room was my bedroom. Late at night I would hear them under my window—they would tell me to lock my door and not to come out, and that if I did they'd show me who was boss.

The nights of anxiety I endured alone are indescribable. There I was, a helpless woman at the mercy of these barbarians. Worse still was the terrible thought that any night my brothers might walk into their trap without my being able to warn them, to be caught and perhaps even shot in cold blood before my very eyes.

Sam and Tryn stayed faithful to me. They were now my only source of help and advice. Tryn slept in my bedroom each night, and Sam ran the farm for me. Strangely enough, the African scouts had a measure of respect for Sam. He warned them not to interfere with me or he would report them to the English. As a result they didn't dare come into the house, but defied me in all sorts of other ways. Sometimes they would arrive in the middle of the day, order young children on the farm to lead their horses around to cool them down, then put them in the stables to be watered and fed. They would strut about the yard as if they owned the place, and they came to the house and ordered Tryn to make them coffee and whatever else they wanted. It was enough to drive one mad, and contributed to a growing realisation that life on the farm was becoming impossible for me. I didn't think I would be able to hold out alone, nor did I think I would be left alone, much longer.

The end was rapidly approaching. I began planning to leave in earnest. One morning I received a letter from the English Commandant at Edenburg, ordering me to come to Edenburg with all my belongings, livestock and all. He accused me of staying on the farm just to cause trouble, of supplying the burghers with food, and of simply being a nuisance to them. I was informed that they would send a wagon in a few days to confiscate the wheat and other goods. This letter gave me a terrible fright, and brought home in no uncertain terms the realisation that I would have to get going immediately, before I could be captured on the farm. How or where to begin was now my biggest problem. I had no one to turn to for advice. When I asked Sam what he thought, he would say, 'What do you think, *nonnie*?'

About one thing I was absolutely certain, however—whatever happened, they were not going to get me. If necessary I would give up everything and flee on my own. I would rather die on a battlefield than in a concentration camp. Spurred on by the fear of being captured, and driven by necessity, my brain worked at speed. Surrender never even occurred to me. All I thought of was escaping with everything I could—the livestock, the wagon, the spider and the wheat.

By the afternoon my plans, for better or worse, were more or less settled. Sam would leave with the sheep, Tryn and Piet would drive the wagon, and I would flee in the spider. But we had no trek oxen. That evening I sent Sam with a letter to the nearest burgher patrol begging them to send trek oxen. I explained my predicament, and that I wanted to keep the wheat out of English hands and leave the railway line behind. The following afternoon

Sam returned with trek oxen, and our preparations began in earnest. We drove the oxen into a camp near the house and started packing. Wheat and other goods were loaded on to the wagon, and everything was readied for the 'Great Trek'.

The following afternoon we were ready, and I asked Sam to bring the oxen closer to be inspanned. Here we encountered a new difficulty. They were an unknown team and we had no idea how they should be inspanned—which were the lead and which the rear oxen. Whichever they were, however, they had to be inspanned and trek. Our first problem was getting hold of the oxen; they hadn't worked for some time, and were lively and boisterous. After a long struggle, and not before a few had slipped their yokes, and a few yoke pins had been broken, we got them inspanned after a fashion. Then Sam helped Piet and Tryn, and after helping me inspan the spider, he rode off to take care of the sheep. I was left alone to say goodbye to the beloved farm.

I walked through the old house from one room to another, bidding farewell and checking that everything was locked. I said goodbye to each room and its furniture before locking the door behind me. The whole house felt sombre and dead. All I could hear was the tick-tock of the clock on the mantlepiece in the living room. I stopped the clock—why should it continue? There was no-one left to keep time for.

I had to hurry. Outside the light was fading, but the remaining light of day couldn't filter the darkness in my soul. I took one last look at the portraits of my dear father and my family, and involuntarily tears came to my eyes. I shut the heavy front door behind me and walked to the spider in which I would travel towards an uncertain future in an alien and bloody world, to God alone knew where.

TWO

With no fixed destination, we chose a direction and trekked away from the farm and the railway line. It was a slow business and the going was difficult. The oxen, which had been inspanned in no particular order, wouldn't pull together. We moved in the direction of Toomfontein. Across the plains behind the mountain came Sam with the flock of sheep. At Toomfontein we waited for them to catch up with us, and I told Sam to trek from there to Vlakfontein, where we would meet up again and make further plans.

At Vlakfontein we rested and camped for about three weeks. It was far from my brothers, and it was not easy taking care of the sheep.

To my great joy my brothers got leave to join Commandant Nieuwoudt's commando. This meant that they were much closer to me—and were able to afford me some protection, while I could assist them with clothing and other provisions. For greater safety and to be closer to them, I trekked from Vlakfontein to Boomplaas, a farm about eight miles away, and about six miles from where my brothers were stationed.

I stayed at Boomplaas for about six weeks, hoping the war would soon be over, for coping with the sheep had become very difficult. It was a large flock, and the wild dogs and jackals were a menace. Also, I felt neither at home nor at ease there. I had a

21

peculiar dread of the big mountains with their deep, dark ravines full of baboons. This was the farm where a battle had taken place in 1848. The officers' graves there and the ghost stories that were told made the place even less attractive to me. Dear old Tryn and the others remained loyal to me, and continued to sleep with me in the house. I also had my faithful dog and the revolver my brothers had given me, so I was at least reasonably protected.

A strange thing happened one night while I was staying there. As usual we locked up the house and went to sleep, but at about eleven o'clock we heard something. Nero, my dog, also heard it and ran growling from one window to the next. I patted and coaxed him so he wouldn't bark. Tryn was afraid, and came to my bed wanting to know what was going on. Suddenly Nero barked loudly and jumped up against the door, and the next thing I knew Tryn was sitting beside me in bed. She wouldn't listen, however much I tried to calm her down, and refused to leave my bed. She insisted that I fire a shot for some kind of reassurance, otherwise she wouldn't budge. There was nothing I could do, so I fired a shot through the door and we sat quietly and listened. When it was all dead quiet again, and nothing had happened, Tryn went, fetched her bedding, and made her bed right next to mine. Thus we spent the rest of the night, without sleeping at all. Early next morning we were anxious to see what had been going on. To our astonishment we found the kitchen door wide open, with the whole lock sawn off, and some of our things stolen from the pantry. So it was a petty thief who had given us such a fright.

It was now my sixth week at Boomplaas, and the experience of the previous night had made me even more afraid of the place. I saw a lot of my brothers. They passed by on their way to blow up the railway line, or when they went out scouting, and they would usually pay me a visit. The morning after the theft I received a message that my brothers would be coming for supper the following evening. Next morning I was up and about early to get everything ready for their arrival, and to prepare a good meal for them.

By afternoon everything was more or less ready, and I went to sit and work in front of the window in my room. I became so engrossed in my needlework that I didn't notice a group of horsemen arriving; and only when they reached the yard did I see that the place was crawling with Khakis. I got such a fright that I simply jumped up to go outside, but before I could do so the English troops came storming into the house and started searching all the rooms. After a while they stopped, but only after they'd stolen what they wanted—that night I didn't even have a slice of bread to eat.

I began to worry less about what was going on at the house— my real concern was what would happen that evening when my brothers arrived as planned. They knew nothing about the enemy, and would therefore ride in, relaxed and ignorant of the danger awaiting them. I had to make a plan. I had to warn them. But how?

The English officers came in, sat in the living room, and called for me. I quickly warned Tryn to say nothing. She was to know nothing of any Boers, nor was she to be able to understand them if they spoke to her. I was still conspiring with Tryn when one of the English again came to tell me that the Commandant wished to see me. When I entered the living room it was full of English soldiers, laughing, chatting and smoking. I had to do everything in my power to control myself. My nerves almost got the better of me. I was afraid, shy and angry, all at the same time. Then the interrogation began.

'What can you tell us about the Boers? ... Where are they? ... Do you see them often? ...' and so on. My interrogator spoke in a quiet and friendly manner, and it didn't seem as if he was going to handle me too roughly.

I said to him, 'Look, it's tea time. Let me first make tea, then

I'll come and sit down and tell you everything.'

My purpose was really to play for time so as to get my plans in order. When I left the room, one of them went and sat down at the piano and began to play *Home, Sweet Home.* It was played so sadly, a cold shiver went down my spine at the sound of the well known melody. Naturally he was thinking of his home, but what about mine? I preferred not to hear it, so I closed the door behind me. After a while the tea was ready, and Tryn took it into the living room. I also went in and stood next to the piano while the playing continued. By now I had a reasonably coherent story in mind. The piano playing stopped, and the Commandant again asked me what I could tell them. I said I knew next to nothing about the Boers, and that I never saw them. But, I told them, there was a patrol of burghers in the area.

'Where, where?' they interrupted me.

I said I didn't know—they never stayed in the same place. I told them that a younger brother of mine was with the burgher patrol, and that he didn't wish to continue fighting. He knew they would never be able to defeat the enemy, and things were so scarce. I was to let him know when an English force arrived as he wished to give himself up and be sent to one of the camps.

'But,' he asked, and here he almost caught me out, 'how would you know where he is if they never stay in the same place?'

'Oh, that's easy,' I answered. 'I write to him often. The letter is placed under a special stone he knows about. He comes and fetches it there, and also leaves one for me.'

I said I was anxious that he should go in under protection, and would like to get my horse and saddle ready to get a message to him. I could write to him now and a young servant could deliver the letter.

The Commandant looked at the others, who seemed to me to be very sceptical and not at all keen on the idea. I approached

24

him, took him by the arm, and in a pleading voice, a half-cry I made sound as pathetic as possible, I begged him to please save my young brother. He spoke to the others again, then said to me, 'All right, write to him in English; then show it to me and I'll see.'

I took some writing paper, went and stood next to him at the piano, and wrote. I was shaking like a leaf and could hardly write, so afraid was I that my plans would backfire. But when the officers started chatting again, my courage returned and I became less timid.

I wrote the following note on the first page of the writing pad:

'Dear Brother

I have promised to let you know; an English convoy has just arrived. Try to come over at once.

Sarah'

Unobserved I lifted up the first page without tearing it off, and wrote on the second page:

'There is a large English force here. They're looking for you. Be careful. Don't come tonight. I've been captured.'

I held out the writing pad so he could read it. My heart was pounding like a hammer in my throat. What would happen to me if he lifted the first page and saw the second? At that moment I couldn't speak. He finished reading and said, 'All right, then, you can send it.'

Ever so carefully, I tore out the two pages together, put them in an envelope, and sealed it in front of them. Only then could I begin to breathe normally again. Once the servant had left everything would be all right—he knew where to find them. Tryn had put him through his paces. He knew the story of the stone

25

post office, and would betray nothing if anyone interrogated him.

The officers all went outside together to watch the servant leave with the letter, and ordered the guards to let him pass. Little did they know he was riding straight to the Boer patrol. Suddenly I felt free and able to relax again. I knew my letter would reach its destination quickly and unharmed. The servant knew the veld, and my brothers were not far away.

After the servant had gone, the Commandant said I must prepare to go with them. They would be leaving early next morning. I then asked him what would become of my belongings.

'Oh, we're taking them!' he said.

'Yes, but then you must give me a receipt for them.'

He agreed to this and gave me a receipt for £1 090, and they burnt the spider. I was very excited and thought to myself, *toe maar*, Khakis, now *you* can struggle to get the sheep out of the mountains—I've got my receipt. I hid the receipt in the hem of a large handkerchief. Luckily they knew nothing about the other money I had on me. Soon I was all packed and ready, for in truth there was almost nothing to pack. The furniture didn't belong to me, and my possessions amounted to just a few little things.

They asked me when my brother was likely to come, and I said I couldn't understand why he hadn't turned up yet. By dusk there was still no sign of the brother who, of course, was never intended to arrive.

Suddenly the Commandant came into the house, and I could hear from his footsteps that something had gone badly wrong. He entered the living room, absolutely livid, and with flaming eyes he sought me out. The moment he saw me he came right up to me, almost poking my eyes out, so close was the finger he pointed in my face. He spat out the words, 'You traitor, I'm going to punish you severely. You might as well prepare yourself to go to gaol.'

I maintained my innocence, and asked him what had

happened. He paid no attention, and continued to abuse me terribly. I was a liar, a traitor, a cheat, he was going to put me in gaol, and so on. He also wanted to take back the receipt he'd given, and said I wouldn't get a single penny. I could see that sweet talk would get me nowhere now, and I was becoming heated at all the abuse he was heaping on me. So I told him I'd placed no value on the receipt he'd given me anyway, and that I'd already burnt it.

I was actually extremely curious to discover what had happened. I called Tryn and found out from her that my brothers had sent a letter back. How they could have done such a foolish thing I cannot to this day understand. In any event, they said in the letter that they would come that evening and teach the Khakis a lesson. On the servant's return, the Khakis took my brothers' letter from him, and that was that. I knew now that my fate was sealed. I could expect only the worst, and prepared myself for Springfontein gaol and its rice water.

That same evening we trekked to the neighbouring farm of Vlakfontein. The next day the Khakis joined battle with the Boer patrol, including my brothers. I could see nothing, but clearly heard the sounds of battle. I sat there, afraid that my brothers might die in the skirmish. They were such a small group, but at least they were sheltered in a good ridge. Late that afternoon, three wounded Khakis were brought back to the convoy. I knew nothing of the outcome of the skirmish and only later asked an officer about the fighting. He answered bitterly, 'You ask as if you don't know. It's all your hellish doing. You'll pay for it. We've shot all your people dead.'

'Where did you bury them?' I asked.

'Bury them! We left them for the wild animals and the vultures!' he answered.

On hearing this shocking news, I turned quietly and climbed back into the tent wagon. Dark shadows were already creeping over the plains, and a feeling of loneliness, homesickness and yearning slowly overcame me. If only it would get dark, I could give vent to my feelings in tears. Later that night I lit my little lamp, simply to sit and contemplate what might lie in store for me. The soldiers repeatedly lifted the canvas and asked why I was not asleep. I sat in silence.

It was a night of distress and fear. Here I was alone in this huge convoy, and somewhere nearby lay my brothers, possibly dead or badly wounded, and I couldn't even be near them to give them some water or attend to their wounds. What would my dear mother think if she knew? And then again, where were she and my dear father? Perhaps also already dead in a camp, where our people were dying like flies, so we heard. And on top of that, my own situation—with the depressing prospect of imprisonment that awaited me. In this fashion I sat and worried the night away, until dawn.

Early next morning I heard women's voices next to the wagon. I peered out to see who it could be, and was almost speechless with surprise. There stood none other than Mrs Metz and Mrs Jacobs, with their children. They'd been taken captive the previous day at Touwfontein, another farm in the same district, and that night they'd been brought on foot to the convoy. My heart went out to them, they looked so thin and exhausted from the long walk.

The next day they sent us to the station at Jagersfontein, and there—without food or water—we sat in an open truck, baking in the hot sun, and in this fashion travelled to Springfontein. On arrival there, we were sent straight to the camp. They put me in a tent with Mrs Jacobs. This wouldn't be for long, I thought to myself, as I still had to go to gaol; and I expected to be fetched at any moment. A few days went by with me expecting to be hauled off to gaol, but nothing happened. I began to take courage and to think they'd forgotten about me. In the meantime I keenly observed all aspects of camp life. It was too much for me, and I realised that I'd never be able to endure it—the wretchedness was indescribable. The death and suffering of people and the terrible conditions they experienced would either drive me insane or be the death of me.

Notwithstanding that things were so awful in the camp, there was nevertheless a section of our people who, unconcerned at the plight of their fellow-Afrikaners, continued living happily and pleasurably. I was astonished to see that Afrikaner girls, not from the camps but those who lived nearby, rode about with English officers and had fun with them, quite clearly without the slightest concern for what was happening on their doorstep.

A few more days went by in this fashion, and nothing happened to indicate that they intended sending me to gaol. I decided to risk a visit to the Commandant. I'd heard that my mother was in Bloemfontein camp, and I hoped to make my way there. I was however afraid, for I was already on the blacklist and could not afford to step further out of line. I asked for an interview with the camp Commandant, and was escorted to his office. When I told him my story, he pointed to a letter on his table and said, 'Oh no, there will be no permission for you. You betrayed us and caused some of our people to be shot. I know all about you. You'll stay in this camp, and not once will your feet step over the perimeter. What is more, you will die here!'

That's what you think, I thought to myself. We would see.

He asked me how many brothers I still had on commando. I said four, and he then began abusing the burghers. 'Those savage Boers, they don't fight, they just go round plundering, robbing and stealing.' My blood grew hotter with each further abuse. Why couldn't I also give vent to my feelings?

So I blurted out, 'No! They are brave men, but what are you— you're a women's Commandant. It's a scandal. There's neither skill nor honour in being a women's Commandant!'

This was too much for him. He jumped up, grabbed me by the chest, shook me a few times, and said, 'Insult me, and you'll find yourself in gaol ... you traitor!'

He turned around suddenly when someone from behind him grabbed his hand. It was a Mr X, the Commandant's secretary. I was more than dumbfounded when I recognised him as one of my teachers during my first years at school. This so-called secretary asked the Commandant to keep calm and proceed more gently. Whether these words had any effect I cannot be sure, for my punishment followed immediately.

I could choose between fourteen days in gaol on rice water, or fourteen days doing the camp guards' washing. I thought for a moment.

'So, what do you say?' shouted the women's Commandant.

'I'll do the washing,' I said calmly, for I had by then already begun to make plans for an alternative solution.

'See that you are here at nine o'clock tomorrow morning,' were the last words of the Commandant. When I walked away contemplating washing the clothes of the filthy Tommies, I was furious. I had to think of a way out of this predicament. Escape seemed the only way of avoiding this business of washing the clothes. Yes, I had to escape from the camp, but how? Even though there wasn't yet a clear opportunity open to me, I was firmly resolved to teach that women's Commandant a lesson.

I went to my tent and came across two of my friends there. I did my very best not to give any indication of my true feelings— I thought it would be unwise to give them too much detail if I wished to obtain their assistance. Had I done so, these two would have been afraid of the punishment they might receive if they helped me escape. So I spoke to them about the impossibility of · camp life, the terrible treatment and the ghastly food we had to put up with, and in this way I led up to the suggestion that we three should attempt an escape.

I suggested that one of them should go and request a pass for herself and her two sisters to fetch wood in the mountains. I would disguise myself so that I could pass for one of the sisters, for I wasn't allowed a step outside the fence. Well, no sooner said than done. They went and requested the pass, while I did the rounds swapping and borrowing to get hold of a *kappie*, spectacles, a sack and an axe. We tried to keep everything very quiet. Nothing must become known—the stakes were too high. I still think that if they'd known about the punishment awaiting me at nine o'clock the next morning, they'd never have dared help me. Before we left, we had to try and get together a few pieces of bread and whatever else could be obtained, and conceal them carefully.

I cannot describe the anxious moments I experienced when we began walking through the camp, closer and closer to the first guard. It was customary for girls and women to go and fetch wood, but this time it was different. My heart was beating in my throat. It felt as if the guards must be aware of our plans. Even the manner in which they looked at us, which on other days we'd have ignored, now looked suspicious.

The first guard read the pass, and looked us up and down a few times. What a relief when I heard the words, 'All right, you may go.'

Then there was a second guard to get past. He looked less suspicious, and as soon as he saw our pass he let us go with a warning not to go anywhere near the ridge as there were some Boers up there. Poor creature, little did he know that that was precisely what we wanted to hear. We were then so eager to get away that it was difficult to walk on in a composed manner, every now and then making as if we were picking up wood, and acting as if that were our only concern.

No sooner were we over the first rise than we threw away our sacks and axes, and ran towards the ridge where the Boers were supposed to be. By the time we were halfway there, my companions were ready to give up the attempt. We'd run as fast as we could and were desperately tired, but I kept on at them not to give up. I had only to think of having to report to the Commandant at nine o'clock the next morning. Eventually we reached the foot of the ridge.

By then we were so exhausted we fell down like three weary horses, trying to regain our breath. We were lying there resting when we heard a voice from somewhere in the ridge, 'You must flee, the English are coming.'

We were paralysed with fear, but soon realised with relief that these were Boers, even though they were wearing khaki. They helped us out of the ridge, and the rest of the Boers, shooting, forced the English back. Risking life and limb, we fled over ridges and through ditches, until that night we reached the farm Ribboksfontein. Mr and Mrs Van Heerden welcomed us heartily, and couldn't stop talking about the daring exploit we three girls had managed successfully. Miss Van Schalkwyk stayed there, for her parents had not yet been taken captive, and she planned to return to them from there.

Springfontein, the first Concentration Camp to which
Sarah Raal was sent and from which she escaped.

THREE

I will never again feel as tired as I did the night we escaped from the Springfontein camp. If ever a bed was welcome and sleep overpowering, it was then. When I awoke with a start the next morning, I was a different person.

I was taken with Miss Jacobs, one of the friends who'd escaped with me, to my brothers at Touwfontein. Their surprise at seeing us was something to behold. They were shaving when we arrived and with their faces still covered in shaving foam they stampeded towards us, kissed us, threw their hats in the air, and shouted, 'Welcome!'

They interrogated us on everything that had happened and there seemed to be no end to their questions. Then came the serious debate about what was to be done with us, as the situation was not looking too rosy. Almost all the houses had been razed to the ground, food was scarce, and things were not likely to go smoothly. At first it was thought that the two of us girls should go and stay wherever there was a house still standing, but in the end it was decided that it would be far safer for us to join the commando than remain alone on a farm, as everyone in the area had been captured and herded off to concentration camps.

Miss Jacobs and I remained together for a while but then we separated, each of us wanting to be with our brothers. That is how I came to join Commandant Nieuwoudt under whom my brothers were serving. General Hertzog joined our commando for a time, and, seeing him at first hand, I could only marvel at his courage, his determination and his unselfish love for his country and his people.

A fair number of strong patrols were sent to the railway line, or rather in the direction of the railway line. My brothers were among those who had to go to Boomplaas and I went with them. I was apprehensive about going there as it was the scene of my previous capture. As I was scared of returning to Boomplaas, we went to stay on Excelsior which was adjacent to Boomplaas. The imposing mountains frightened me—they looked so mysterious and full of unknown danger that I felt as if some misfortune might befall us at any moment. But I was now part of the struggle, and I had no choice in the matter. It was too dangerous for us even to sleep in the houses. Every evening we would seek out a safe kloof where we could set up camp. We had a scout out at all times because we were moving very close to the English route, and every now and then we had them under fire. We could not allow them to discover where we were based. Unfortunately we couldn't attack the large English columns, for our commando was split into small groups and we had limited supplies of ammunition, something the English were all too aware of. Yet, despite everything, they were wary of us because they knew that when it came to a shootout, they would not escape unscathed.

One fine evening we were preparing to ride out for the night when my brother Abram told me he was feeling unwell, and would not be able to ride far that night. He'd been out on patrol all day and had probably had too much sun. His body ached, and he had a very high temperature. We decided that the two of us would spend the night on a large ridge behind the house, and that my horse would remain saddled in the stables. If anything were to happen I would be able to come down from the ridge and fetch my horse while he saddled his, and we could then flee to the other burghers, as I knew where they were sleeping.

After the others had left we climbed the ridge to find a safe place to sleep. Abram lay down immediately as he was feeling terrible. But I could not sleep. Next to me lay my younger brother, just eighteen years old and already hardened. What would my mother say if she could see him lying here on the hard ground, on his face a look that made one suspect the worst? I couldn't help wondering why fate had singled me out to have to witness all these terrible things.

I waited in vain for sleep to come—but there was no repose for me, and I felt a strange restlessness. Could it be my brother's illness? I put on my leggings and sat up. What time was it, I wondered. The moon, which was particularly bright, was already high in the heavens. Were those horses' hooves I could hear or was I imagining it? Could it be the Boers? I couldn't work out where they were coming from.

I woke my brother and told him I could hear horses' hooves. He listened a while, then told me I was imagining it. He turned over and went back to sleep. But I didn't trust the quiet. I listened with all my might and distinctly heard the clip-clop of horses' hooves—indeed, I could actually see the horsemen in the moonlight.

I shook Abram gently and whispered to him that the English were close by. He peered carefully through the bushes.

'*Ja, wragtie*, so they are, and they're taking up position in front of the house and in the ditch. Let's get out of here,' he whispered. But he pulled me back at once, saying he first wanted to go and fetch my horse from the stables. His horse was hobbled in the veld. I wouldn't hear of it, for the English were all over the house and the yard, and they'd almost certainly capture and shoot him.

'No they won't,' he said. 'I'm also wearing khaki, remember. I'll be able to walk among them and they'll think I'm one of them. You creep to the foot of the hill and wait for me there until I bring your horse. Then you can ride to the commando and I'll follow on foot.'

Try as I might to tell him it was folly, and that we should rather both flee on foot to the commando where there were sufficient extra horses, he wouldn't listen.

I started creeping down the hill on my hands and knees while he went to the stable to fetch my horse. I had to proceed carefully or they might see me, but eventually I reached the foot of the ridge, my hands and knees bleeding and my dress torn to shreds. Now all I could do was sit and wait for my brother. I could hear nothing, and everything was eerily quiet. Suddenly I felt a cowardly urge to run away, but then I remembered my brother's sick, pallid face, and considered the risk he was running for me. No, I could never leave him behind alone.

He, meanwhile, had crept down the ridge until he was a short distance from the house. Then he stood up and walked towards it. The Tommies didn't bat an eyelid, for, dressed as he was in khaki, he looked just like one of them in the moonlight. Next to the house stood a large tank, and there he sat washing his hands while one of the Tommies tapped water from the tank. Cool as a cucumber he walked to the stables, waited his chance, then led my horse quietly away. While I was still standing there worrying, he arrived with my beloved horse. Just then the moon disappeared behind a cloud and I was able to mount without being seen. Unfortunately, however, my horse was white, and as I set off I was showered with bullets. In his haste my brother had not tightened the girth properly, but there was no time for me to stop and do so now. I let my horse gallop as fast as he could despite the fact that my saddle was moving from side to side on his back. Fortunately he was a calm horse and it made no difference to him where I sat on his back.

Despite these difficulties I eventually reached the Boers, told them what had happened, and said they should take a horse to my brother. Luckily, however, he'd managed to get hold of his horse and arrived not long after I did. He told us the English had already taken up position so that when we returned the following morning they'd be waiting for us. It was a blessing that my brother and I had chosen to sleep where we did, or I'd probably have been captured a second time and would then certainly have had to spend the remainder of the war in a prison cell.

An order came for us to move to a ridge directly in front of us, to prevent the enemy from encircling us before morning. By sunrise we were safely in the bush covered ridge, and from there we could keep a good watch on the English without them being able to see us.

Morning was just breaking when we spotted two riders coming directly towards us, completely unaware of the danger they were in. When they got closer we saw that they were an officer and an African. As we later discovered, the officer was on his way to the English column and the African was there to show him the way. To our great delight, they'd lost their way during the night and were contentedly heading straight for us.

When they were almost on top of us, a couple of burghers stood up and shouted, 'Hands up!'

We heard the African say to the Englishman, 'Sir, put up your hands, it's the Boers.'

But he readied his rifle and shouted, 'Are you mad? Can't you see I'm one of your officers?' He also gave his name, which we didn't catch. Of course he'd mistaken the burghers in their khakis for English. Our men shot to kill his horse so that they could 'shake him out'—send him back to his own people minus rifle, horse, uniform or boots. They shot and killed the African's horse and wounded the officer in the side. It was a very minor injury, just sufficient to serve as a small reminder of the war.

All anyone could think about now was gathering their

belongings because the English, who were just on the other side of the ridge, must have heard the shots and they would now be aware that their work of the previous evening had been in vain. Any minute they were bound to start making life difficult for us. We placed the officer on his horse, and told the African to lead him round the ridge where he would find the English. Then we left and travelled as far as Sleutelspoort, where we took up position in the ridges. It wasn't far from the English troops for we could watch their every movement through the binoculars. I then took some time to put on another dress and bandage my hands and knees as I was the only 'casualty' among us. The burghers teased me saying I should be satisfied because they'd punished the English officer for the discomfort of my injured hands and knees, and he was probably in hospital by now while I was still able to flee.

I vowed to myself that I would never return to Boomplaas, and to my great relief the burghers decided that we would move to Transvalie, at the foot of the mountain there. The mountain was high and we could easily keep watch in every direction. Here we remained—peacefully one day, at war the next. The enemy had many advantages over us. They had sufficient food, trek animals, and ammunition, and enough Afrikaners and Hottentots to give them information about our secret hiding places. As a result we had to be particularly vigilant, especially at night; and if it rained and we spent the night in a house, we always had a good patrol out keeping watch.

One lovely, clear Sunday our scouts were out on the highest kopje, and we were spending the day quietly seeing to our clothes, thinking the English would be similarly engaged. At about eleven o'clock one of the burghers, Attorney Brand, announced that he wanted to go to Excelsior to see if he could find any of our things there, for when we'd had to flee in the middle of the night we'd left our belongings behind and they'd been burnt by the English. Brand left, and those Boers who were not seeing to their clothes were lying around relaxing in the sun. Brand was gone for scarcely twenty minutes when he arrived back in an agitated state, carrying an Englishman's helmet. He told us the road was covered in fresh hoof prints, and while the words were still coming from his mouth, along came our scout.

'*Opsaal kêrels*, Excelsior is crawling with English,' he shouted.

They'd probably come past during the night, which was why our patrol hadn't seen them. And they probably thought we were still there. There was nothing for it but to gather our belongings and saddle up.

There being only about twenty of us, we had to avoid a pitched battle. We set off in the direction of a farm called Buffelbout, but we'd gone scarcely a thousand yards when we saw a whole company of mounted troops to our left. They seemed in no great hurry to attack us. Indeed, they allowed us to continue diagonally in front of them despite the fact that they were heading in the same direction. We had no choice but to continue in that direction, although we had no idea what was going to happen. If they were not careful we would get to the ridge before them and then we'd be in a favourable position. At an estimate there were about three hundred of them, but we nevertheless thought we could take them on provided we had good cover. Alas, however, their cunning soon emerged—a large English force, armed with cannons, appeared out of nowhere on our right. We couldn't retreat because we were between two walls of the enemy, and for the rest it was just one long, open plain. All we could do was try to get to the ridge directly in front of us.

Three burghers dashed back. A shell went off under one of their horses, and the uninjured rider jumped up behind one of his comrades as bullets and shells rained down around us. I was unfortunately not riding my favourite horse, which I liked to spare as much as possible for difficult days—and I hadn't imagined that that day would turn out the way it did. My brother was leading my horse and I was riding an inferior little pony. Before I knew it the pony was exhausted. I shouted to my brother that my horse was finished and there and then, amid the clatter of bullets, we had to change saddles, which resulted in us falling somewhat behind the others. My courage seemed ready to desert me at any moment as the shells screeched overhead, and wherever we looked we saw bullets tearing into the veld. I don't think I was so much scared of dying as of being captured again, in which case they would probably torture me to death anyway.

We reached the ridge safely, and some of the burghers had already started shooting back. When we got to the top of the ridge we could see a wagon pulled by a team of black oxen charging as fast as it could across the plains, with a couple of Tommies in hot pursuit. It was a group of poor women who'd been fleeing from place to place, but who were eventually captured that day. Where we were now they couldn't shoot us, but their horsemen were bound to catch up with us soon. However, we had to rest our horses before fleeing further.

While we were standing there one of the burghers came riding up to us. He looked deathly pale, his horse had been shot dead under him, and he'd had to continue on his loaded pack horse. As he came past, he shouted at the top of his voice that we must stop the horse, which was running away with him, as he couldn't stop it. Despite the circumstances, we had to laugh, for although he kept telling us to stop the horse, he continued hitting it which of course had the opposite effect! The poor animal was completely confused for the man should have been sitting on top of the pack of blankets strapped to its back, but these had slipped round to between its legs, and it kept stepping on them.

Down the ridge we went to Rus-in-Vrede, where we knew our

own men to be. The English had also reached the top of the ridge and were about seven or eight hundred paces behind us. Wherever we looked there were bullets. We couldn't move as quickly as we'd been moving, for our horses were tired. Luckily the English didn't come down the ridge, but kept shooting at us from above. Suddenly I heard the voice of my brother, Jacobus, riding next to me, say, 'I've been wounded, but don't stop, just ride on.'

When I looked at him my heart wanted to break. His face was deathly pale, and there was blood streaming from his mouth and nose. I took out my water bottle and gave it to him. By this time it was getting dark, and we rode just a little further before stopping to see to his wound. He'd been shot through the right shoulder. After we'd done all we could, we moved on towards Commandant Nieuwoudt's laager which we knew had to be close by. We even thought that they must have heard the shooting and might come to our aid. We soon arrived, but as there was no doctor I had to do my best to keep the wound clean with tepid water, and open so that it could heal on the inside.

We decided to stay with the laager, which usually kept to the western side of the Free State. Life was exhausting: food was scarce, we had little ammunition, the world around us was destroyed, and some towns and farms were utterly deserted, with everyone either captured or on commando. The English had said, 'Let us capture the women, burn the farms, and destroy the livestock; then we'll have won the war.'

The morning after joining the laager we moved to Jagersfontein. The first place we stopped at was Heneweerskop in the Fauresmith district. Our patrol went out that night, and everything went peacefully and well. The next day was windy and miserable—it was on such days more than others that I longed for home, by now perhaps burnt to the ground, and for my family who, for all I knew, might be dead. My uncle, Field-

Cornet Lubbe, his son Andries, who was only twelve years old, my two brothers and I were sitting behind a big broom bush. The ridges we were on formed a crescent and we were on one point of the crescent. My uncle said he didn't feel well. He wasn't sick but felt uneasy, and he had a particular longing for his wife and children. He gave me his watch and told me to give it to his wife one day. While he was busy taking it off his arm we heard the order, 'Field-cornet, you and your men must storm the ridge; the enemy is reaching the summit.'

What our patrol had been up to that night I do not know. Under cover of darkness the English had moved into the hills, and they knew we were on the other side of the hill, but they didn't want to attack us as they were waiting for reinforcements from Jagersfontein. We then moved to the other end of the ridge, on the far side of the crescent, while my uncle and his men moved into position to attack the English coming from Jagersfontein. The English who'd climbed the ridge during the night were shooting at the Boers positioned at the bottom of the ridge.

FOUR

It was a short skirmish, but one of the bloodiest I ever saw. We sat on the other ridge watching the fight. Two of our burghers had been captured. Then my uncle was wounded. He was shot through the hip, and the Commandant told him to ride away. Behind a rock lay one of the burghers and near him, behind another, lay an African. The burgher was ready to shoot should the African raise his head. My uncle, who knew nothing about this, galloped between them. Just as he did so the burgher fired and my uncle was hit in the heart, falling from his horse. His young son Andries, who was with us, became hysterical, and we had to restrain him from running to his father. Two more burghers were injured, but there were no further fatalities. Of the English seventeen were dead and many wounded, and the burghers had captured their horses and rifles by the time the fighting was over.

Then we had to establish whether or not my uncle was dead. My younger brother Abram and another young man, Roux, said they would go and check. They'd not gone fifty yards when they were peppered with bullets, but they made it safely and saw that he was indeed dead. They took his horse, which was still standing next to him, and his rifle, and galloped back. His horse, saddle and bridle were given to his son.

We moved a short distance before stopping to take care of the wounded. This was usually a difficult task as we could use no light for fear of betraying our whereabouts, and it was very difficult to treat wounds in the dark. We made a sort of screen by tacking blankets together with thorns. A few burghers then stood and held these to allow enough room inside. They stood on the blankets so as not to allow even the faintest glimmer of light to escape and betray us. Sometimes we were short of candles, and then we had only the light of matches in which to work with the wounded. When we finished we had to carry the wounded in blankets because they couldn't endure the bumping of the wagon. We moved off in the direction of Slagkraal, and arrived there at first light the next day.

The wounded had to be treated in a section of the house that was still standing. A few of the burghers, my brother, whose wound had not yet healed, my cousin Andries, who was still grieving and weeping about his father, and I stayed in the house. Commandant Nieuwoudt set up camp a short distance away, but close enough to be able to see what was happening at the house. During the night there was little chance of sleep as the wounded moaned and groaned, wanting first this, then that. Morning had just broken when Commandant Nieuwoudt ordered the wounded to be put in the back of the wagon and sent off. He ordered the rest of us to flee.

The English had surrounded us during the night. Before we knew what had happened, the house was showered with bullets and we had to catch and saddle our horses under deadly fire. Commandant Nieuwoudt told me I could choose for myself whether I wanted to make a run for it or hide until the wounded had gone, after which they would return and provide cover to enable me to escape, for it didn't look as if there were very many English. But I wouldn't hear of it. Imagine if Gosling, the 'women Commandant', got his hands on me! What a terrible thought! So I told the men I wanted to ride with them, and that if I was shot and killed they should ask the English for my body, take the money I still had on me, and give it to my parents.

On the stoep of the house we saddled up and prepared to ride out, all at the same time. First off was the wagon carrying the wounded. They almost died, poor things, because there was no way to steer and the two mules pulling the wagon just ran through the veld—all the bumping and shaking must have driven them half mad with pain.

Bullets rained down on us as we rode out from the stoep. Despite the fact that we lay as low as possible on our horses, I still felt as if I might get a bullet in my back at any moment. I felt my horse give way under me, and when I came to I was lying on the ground. It all happened so quickly that my companion was two hundred yards ahead of me before he realised that I wasn't there. Luckily I wasn't injured, and when I looked round to see what had caused my fall, I saw my horse had got both his front feet stuck in an aardvark hole. I jumped up, grabbed the bridle, and got him out of the hole. By the time my companion looked round to see if I was wounded or dead, I was back on my horse galloping as fast as I could to escape the line of fire.

Once we were all safe again we decided to go and scare the Khakis a little. This caused the English to fall back immediately as there weren't many of them, and from this we deduced that their main body must be close by and that they were probably on our trail. It certainly looked as if the enemy didn't want to give us any peace. So we decided to head in a completely different direction, as we needed time to rest. Our horses' legs were finished, the injured burghers' wounds had had no opportunity to heal with all the moving about, and we ourselves were exhausted.

In front of us lay a long line of ridges and we wanted to move through them, but we weren't at all sure where the English troops were located. For all we knew they might already be in the ridges. There was a long endless plain to be crossed, and if they were in the ridges they would allow us to get up close and only then let loose their cannon fire at us, exposed on the open veld. That would undoubtedly be the end of us.

I called the Commandant and said to him, 'Commandant, lend me your binoculars and I'll ride to the ridge. I can scout there, and see what's going on. If all is safe I'll raise a white handkerchief, and if you don't see anything you'll know the English have captured me.'

'We'll never shelter behind you, especially when you're so scared of being recaptured,' he retorted.

'But, Commandant,' I repeated, 'they won't shoot me if they capture me—all they'll do is send me back to the camp. Our animals are finished. We have to come up with a plan, and I'm determined to go.'

He then said I mustn't blame him if it didn't go well with me, and that he wasn't going to lend me his binoculars as he'd then be without them if they captured me. I asked him to organise another pair for me. My brothers were greatly opposed to my going, but I told them I'd already made up my mind. Then they insisted that I give them the money because the English would only take it from me if I was captured, but I wouldn't hear of it.

I mounted my horse and quickly rode out to the ridge. When I was some distance away the commando started to move. They came slowly, hanging back far enough so they could easily turn tail and flee if something went wrong.

When I reached the bottom of the ridge I stopped and studied it through the binoculars. I was so terrified that every stone and bush looked like an Englishman to me. I was actually shivering on my horse, and called myself a fool for ever risking such a thing. I wanted nothing more than to turn round, but pride and the thought that the burghers would think me a coward made me ride some distance up the ridge. There I halted, and proceeded on legs that could scarcely carry me a step further. Finally I reached the top. I promptly sat down and got out the binoculars. I concentrated, looking in all directions to see if I could see anything, listening to hear if I could hear anything, when suddenly a steenbok jumped out of the bush next to me. I fell off the stone I was sitting on, legs in the air, but nevertheless shouted, 'Hands up!' After a while I started looking for my revolver, and my only comfort was that the burghers would thankfully never know of my embarrassment. I didn't want them to lose their good opinion of me.

I picked up the binoculars and looked carefully round once more, but saw nothing. Then I broke a stick off one of the broom bushes, tied a white handkerchief to it, and waved to the burghers. They saw it quickly and hurried to the ridge. When they arrived it was decided to let the horses rest there until late that afternoon, while the scouts went off to find a safe place for us to rest for a few days.

We were hungry, for food was very scarce. The occasional cow or sheep we came across was so wild that we had to shoot from a distance. We had hardly any clothes left on our bodies, and our ammunition was getting dangerously low as time went by. It was a struggle to endure it all, and still to keep going and maintain courage.

That evening it was decided to split the commando. Two groups would move in different directions in order to confuse the enemy, for they had about twelve to fourteen companies in convoy. Breaking through their line would not be easy as their horses were well fed, and they had plenty of food and ammunition, while we were particularly badly off in these respects. They fought when it suited them, took plenty of rest, had enough doctors and nurses, and there were more than enough 'joiners' and Hottentots to guide them, and to locate and reveal our hiding places.

Our large commandos were now mainly in the Transvaal and in the Cape Colony. After our commando divided, the group I was with moved up the ridge because somewhere ahead was a convenient place where both we and our horses could rest for a while. If only we could get our hands on some food! I had a few pieces of biltong which I had looked after very well, for in our desperate circumstances you really couldn't blame anyone for stealing food, and if anyone so much as saw your mouth moving, they would ask what you were eating and whether they could have some. So we had to eat the few scraps we could find in stealth.

That same day we captured a Khaki-Boer on a fat horse. His legs were bound and he was wearing khakis—a real traitor. We took him some way with us and gave him nothing to eat. First he had to get really hungry. Then a couple of burghers stayed behind with him while the rest of us continued on our way. They wanted to 'shake him out'—send him into the blue yonder minus rifle, horse, clothing or boots. What happened to him after that I don't know, but I do know that the stripes on his back and his empty stomach would make him think twice before betraying the Boers again.

At about midnight we arrived at our intended place of rest. Here the mountains formed a sort of crescent and, after our scouts had been deployed, we rested as it looked safe and there was plenty of food and water for us and the animals. At eight o'clock the next morning the scouts were relieved, and everything still seemed safe. We then set about looking for food. Some went off to shoot game, and by afternoon we were all busy cutting biltong and hanging it in the trees so that it could at least be wind-dry before we had to move on. Wherever you looked you saw groups of Boers sitting around fires with pieces of meat on sticks, cooking them over their fires. The meat was scarcely pale on the outside when it was cut off with a knife and devoured; then more meat was held over the fire in the same way. All the leftover meat was stuffed into our saddle bags, for who knew when we might

48

have to set off and where would we again find meat this easily?

That night we had to move on. The plan was to go to Kalbasdrif, where there were high mountains that could provide shelter and rest for some ten or twelve days. It started raining heavily, and it was so dark you couldn't see the person next to you. We struggled on, and every so often someone would call 'Halt!' That usually meant that the ambulance had fallen into a ditch or was stuck in the mud. Oh, what a terrible night that was. If anyone had told me I would live through such times I wouldn't have thought it possible, but the longing for freedom, a deep empathy with our people suffering in the camps, and the blood of the Afrikaner nation flowing for freedom and justice, inspired us to continue.

I often felt pleased that my parents knew nothing of how hard things were for me, for they'd brought me up in a refined and Christian way, and it would have broken their hearts to see me in shredded clothes, tanned brown, and thin from hunger. If only they were still alive we could make a new beginning together after the end of the war. I was still young and could be of great assistance, and my brothers could once again ease the burden of farming for my father. The thought of them dying in a concentration camp and being buried like dogs, wrapped in a khaki-blanket, used to drive me mad.

We kept going until daybreak. It grew light and, believe it or not, we found we'd arrived at a farmhouse. We immediately started drying our clothes, and again began preparing a meal. The sun had been up a while, the food was ready, and we were eating out of our konkas, as we called the cooking tins. Suddenly bullets rained down on us! Konkas, food and all, went flying through the air, and the order came, '*Opsaal*! Head for the ridge!' Thus the stillness of a Free State morning was shattered.

Confusion reigned. We were hungry, cold, and alarmed. Some burghers fled to the ridge on foot, some on horseback, the enemy peppering us with fire. Luckily the ridge wasn't far from the farm buildings, and soon we were all there. The English stormed the ridge, but we were reasonably sheltered, while they were exposed on the open plain, and the Boers were shooting for all they were worth. The English were close enough for us to shout 'Hands up!' An English officer was shot dead no more than twenty yards from me, and a few others besides. That scared them off somewhat, and they set about removing the wounded. Then came the order that we should move along the side of the mountain. Those burghers whose horses were still strong would stay behind to keep the enemy at bay should they attack again.

My horse was still strong because I had two: I rode Mick most of the time, and saved Tiekie for the difficult days. I sent Mick, who had a saddle sore on his back, ahead with the burghers, and I stayed behind with Tiekie. I was ordered to move on with the burghers, but I wouldn't hear of it. My horse was fit and I preferred to remain with those who stayed behind. To be honest, I was afraid of moving on with the weaklings.

By now the English were wary of us, and when we saw a group of our own men making their way in the distance behind a large ridge, we decided to head in the same direction. They were moving quickly, and we struggled to catch up with them. I heard one of the burghers mutter, '*Magtie*, look at that commando move; it just shows you what a thin horse can do under a terrified rider!'

When we caught up with them there was no time to eat or dry our clothes, as we had to keep moving that night. The ambulance wagon had been left behind in the fighting, and the wounded burghers were now on horseback. We struggled on with great difficulty. About halfway to our destination, we suddenly heard the sound of something. We stopped, dead quiet, listening carefully. It was horses' hooves. We lay flat on our horses so as not to be seen. Luckily the night was very dark, and the riders passed by entirely unaware of our close presence. We came to the top of a kopje, and on the other side saw the fires of a host of encamped English troops. We pulled up immediately and moved off as quietly and as quickly as possible. There were hardships all the way, with one horse after another giving in, the rider having to carry his saddle and bridle, and others refusing to move another step. Somehow we reached our destination, Kalbasdrif, by sunrise. Now we had merely to monitor the movements of the English troops. Surely they wouldn't come and bother us here— they had only been in the mountains once, and we now had an excellent view on all sides. There was moreover plenty of water, as a river ran through the mountains. But the prospect of finding food didn't look good. That reminded me of the wet biltong in the saddlebags, which had to be hung out to dry immediately. On the banks of the river there was good soil, lots of shrubs and thorn trees, and plenty of broom bushes to hide behind. If our scouts did their job properly, both we and our animals would be able to have a good rest here. We had also seen the spoor of cattle and sheep, so there had to be something hereabouts to hunt. The first day we saw nothing, but on the second day we spotted a few goats on a cliff high in the mountains. Nobody could get to them, but even if one could have climbed up there, they were very wild and it would have been impossible to get close enough to make a kill. A few burghers took their rifles and shot at them. As the burghers moved down, two of the goats came down from the cliffs as well. Halfway down they must have got stuck because they stopped. In a flash one of our men climbed back up and herded them down further. When they came within range, they were skilfully shot—and at last we could celebrate and still have something over to save as biltong.

I always looked after my hunting bag. Countless times the Commandant had sidled up to me and said, 'How's it going, soldier, any chance of a spare piece of biltong for a hungry Commandant? I must be on my way, and I'm sick and tired of braaied meat.' The burghers were very good to me, and each of them would always bring me a morsel—which meant I could always put something away. Some of the biltong was very thinly sliced so that it would dry quickly; while some was very sinewy and difficult to eat.

We stayed put for ten days, and everyone did as he pleased as each man was his own boss for the time being. It was while we were thus camped that I truly longed for peace, and wondered whether our people would ever be free again, and whether we would ever again live at home as families. Where would the money come from, and who would have the courage to start all over again? When would things ever again progress as far as they had before the war started? When I had thoughts like these, I felt the urge for revenge; and at such times I was unafraid of shooting to kill. I was too depressed about our devastated country, and the fact that we would have to start again from the beginning.

The men noticed that I'd become quiet and withdrawn after the depressing conversation we'd had the previous evening. It had rattled me completely, and made me realise just how much the burghers had sacrificed for their freedom. How many of them had lost the best years of their lives for studying? How many of them had sacrificed good positions and a good living? Could the sacrifice ever be repaid? One of the burghers said, '*Kêrels*, we're still young, and still have many years ahead of us. We won't be weaker than our forefathers, who had not only the English but also the Kaffirs and wild animals to contend with.'

'*Ja, my nefie*,' answered a grey haired older man, 'you are still young. Your future lies ahead of you. You can start over again if you have to. But what about we who are older, whose best years lie behind us? Where do we find the courage to start all over again?' Two large tears ran down his cheeks, and he stood up and walked off into the bushes.

That night, it seemed, we'd all been thinking about the future that looked so bleak, and we were all very subdued. Then one of the men jumped up and said we couldn't go on like this, that we had to get some life in us, that we had to do something to cheer ourselves up. He suggested that we stage a concert in order, as he put it, to prevent our talents and manners from getting rusty. He told each of us what we had to do, and the show went on. Some had to sing songs—usually those who couldn't sing at all—while others had to recite verse. Actually, it was great fun. There was, however, one man who wouldn't do a thing. He sat on one side watching, and after each performance he would say, '*Ou Bees!*' That was the sum total of his contribution to the concert.

Later Commandant Nieuwoudt, who also took part in the concert, said it was time to send out the scouts. Although it was reasonably safe where we were, we had to have scouts. He chose two youngsters who were very inexperienced and skittish. Our commando had moved to the other side of the mountain where we could keep better watch over the railway line. The boys went off, and after we'd organised everything, we went to sleep. At about two o'clock that morning we were woken by the clatter of horses' hooves. The two youngsters were riding towards us, shouting, '*Opsaal*, Commandant, an armoured train is coming this way, it's coming along the old road, and it's got a terrible big red eye!' A few of the burghers went up the ridge to check things out. They saw nothing, and all we could imagine was that the scouts had seen a train which, as it came round the bend, looked as if it were coming along the road—which made them think it was indeed coming along the old road.

Sometimes such amusing incidents happened that one couldn't help laughing. I remember one man who tied his horse to the back wheel of one of the wagons and fed him there, so that in the event of danger he wouldn't have to look for his horse. Not unnaturally, an ox was attracted to the food and sidled up to the horse. The ox must have frightened the horse, for the horse pulled himself free and thundered off into the night. That night the scouts galloped into the camp shouting, '*Opsaal*! The English are coming!' The man went straight for his horse. It was raining, and so dark you couldn't see your hand in front of you. With one leap the man vaulted onto the back of his 'horse,' and then the fun started. The ox kicked and jumped and went berserk, but no matter how much the man hit and coaxed it, there was no chance of him getting away. After all the other burghers were gone, we could still hear the man saying, '*Ag, Here,* animal, you're not an ox you know!'

One of the burghers who had stayed behind saw what was happening and shouted to the man, 'What's the matter with you, you must go. What are you doing on the back of that ox?'

The Commandant came to me one day and told me it was time for us to move on, for our horses were refreshed and the men were getting restless. They wanted to go and fight. When I asked him what we would fight with, as our ammunition was almost finished, the Commandant said we would have to capture ammunition from the English. One of the men interrupted, saying, '*Janee*, we must go and fight. If the English do take our country, we must at least make them leave a few large pools of blood behind, so that in time to come we can know our enemy by them.'

The Commandant then ordered us to trek in the direction of the railway line. The railway line, where it was so dangerous! But this time I really didn't care. I too had the urge to fight, even though I recognised this as just big talk. In the heat of battle I would often laugh and cry at the same time, to fool my brothers—who worried about me so much—that there was no fear in me, for I never wanted to hinder the burghers by showing my fear. When in danger I usually sheltered my body as best I could, and after the battle I would speak as one who'd been in the thick of the fight.

That day one of our scouts was shot dead by two Africans.

The whole commando mourned Japie's death. He was such a good man and had fought so well. When Japie was out scouting, we knew that nothing would go wrong. His companion had shot back at the Africans, but they were well away by then. It was already dark, but we packed and saddled up in a fury, intent upon pursuing the Africans and punishing them.

We knew more or less where they were to be found, and rode through the night until we came upon the English camp next morning. All was absolutely quiet, with only the occasional fire burning. They were camped beside a river in thick bush. The river (the Riet River) was full, which favoured us as we could encircle them in the bush and they would not be able to escape across the river. We hoped the two Africans were with them.

By the time the English saw us bullets were raining down on them. They were so taken by surprise that they were unable to shoot back, and it was only here and there that an English shot rang out. We had only to think of Japie to fight with determination. I stayed bunched with the men, and shot left and right at the Africans I saw. The English abandoned everything, including their weapons, and fled in any direction as quickly as they could. We captured about a hundred of them, who told us they were about a hundred and seventy strong.

Meanwhile our men were still shooting into the bush, for who knew how many of the enemy might still be lurking there. Commandant Nieuwoudt shouted that they should come out and give themselves up. Suddenly one of them emerged from the bush and, with the hot fire from the Boers continuing unabated, he was soon hit by a bullet right in the forehead. When he fell, another soldier rushed out and didn't even concern himself about us. He knelt next to the wounded man, wiping the blood off him with a handkerchief and saying, 'Oh, I promised mother I'd look after you, what am I to do now?' With that all my joy disappeared, and I cried with the Englishman. They were both so young and looked so innocent. The Boers told the survivor to return to his own men.

But the fun was not yet over. The Boers now began to 'shake out' the English troops—sending them off minus rifle, horse, uniform and boots. There was one strange character with us who would always storm the enemy, grab an Englishman and, emerging with him, shout to us, 'Come on, *kêrels*, I've already got mine!' He would 'shake out' his Englishman, then position himself on a stone or ant-heap to watch the rest of the Boers in action.

The sun had been up for some time now, and we had to make plans to get away, for we had no idea how many English there were behind the ridges. Among the group we had captured were five Africans. The Boers encircled them and told them they would all be shot dead if they didn't say which of them had been out scouting on the ridge where Japie had been killed the previous evening. The Africans were so cunning that we had to resort to guile to get them to talk. None wished to open his mouth. So the Boers started loading and readying their weapons. After a while the Africans were ashen, and eventually one of them could hold out no longer. He jumped up and pointed out the two Africans who'd been there. At length one of the two admitted he'd been there, but said his companion—who finally confessed to it—had shot Japie. The companion was then taken to a ridge, and Japie's death was avenged.

We took rifles, horses, food and clothing from the English we'd captured, abandoned them to their fate, and made our getaway. Before we left I told a few English that they were a gang of land thieves, and that they should make sure I never caught up with them again. One asked me if I was a general, to which I answered 'Yes,' with a straight face.

We rested well for the rest of the day, and inspected our booty. Some of the rifles we hid in the ridge because we couldn't take everything with us. On the farm where we found ourselves, we discovered a very fresh grave, but there was not a living soul around, so we had a look to see who it was that was buried there. Predictably, we found several shells in the grave, which we in turn buried elsewhere.

One of the burghers went on about ghosts on the farm, and no matter how much I protested that we should sleep elsewhere, they wouldn't hear of it. The house alone was enough to give one the cold shivers. It was a large house, but there was not a single door or window remaining. The English had used them all as firewood. Around the house was one stretch of bush after another. There was a maze of spider webs inside, and the wind howled through the house. Yes, such was the place we'd chosen to celebrate the morning's brilliant victory.

We weren't allowed to use any light, which hardly mattered as we didn't have a single candle between us, so we made our beds by feeling our way around in the dark. Our section, being my two brothers, my uncle, his son and I, chose a room close to the front door. I lay between my two brothers, but it didn't help at all. I was still frightened, and they didn't seem to me to be altogether at ease themselves. Suddenly we heard some of the burghers in one of the other rooms shouting, 'Here he is, *kêrels*, watch out!' And before we knew what was going on, a group of wild cats ran through the door to our room, right over us, and out at the window. They disturbed our sleep throughout the night. Some of the burghers went to sleep on the stoep to get away from the cats. I nearly suffocated that night as I lay with my head under the blanket the entire time. We left early the next morning, and never have I felt so pleased to leave a place behind.

Again we had to check our weapons, count our ammunition, and stuff dried meat into our saddle bags. Once everything was in order we moved off in the direction of Jagersfontein. The business area was dead quiet, and there was not a soul to be seen. We, of course, looked for what we needed, and found a good deal. The houses were still furnished as before. One of our burghers went to look for clothes in one of them. He was being careful, though, and kept turning round to check that everything was all right. Once when he looked up he saw a man standing next to him. He whipped out his pistol and shot him. The others heard the shot and stormed into the room. All we saw was that one of the mirrors on the cupboard had been shot to pieces—he'd obviously seen and shot at his own reflection in the mirror.

Our Commandant came to tell us that we should divide into even smaller groups. He'd heard from one of our patrols that the English were coming, and since they invariably moved about in a great host, we would have to form smaller groups to get through their lines. The terrain was also littered with English spies. They were probably thinking that, come what may, no Boer would get through to the railway line. It almost looked as if they were planning to hem us in. My brothers and I went off with fifteen other burghers. When we were a short distance from Jagersfontein, we came across the first English troops. There were lights wherever you looked, as if the whole world were on fire, and we were supposed to get through this! We stayed as close to each other as possible and rode slowly and carefully, so they wouldn't hear our horses' hooves. My two brothers were riding next to me. They said that if the English started shooting, I must flee. Luckily we knew the surrounding territory well.

The English remained ignorant of our presence, and by sunrise next day we were once more on Boomplaas. Here we waited to discover what the enemy's plans might be. There were now just two farms between us and the railway line, and if the English pushed us in that direction it would be the end of us. We fifteen could do nothing against their superior numbers. We therefore decided to return to our own farm.

FIVE

At about three o'clock that afternoon we reached Toomfontein, the farm bordering on my father's farm. There we climbed a kopje, and looked to see what was happening on Boomplaas. The place was crawling with Tommies. Between Toomfontein and our farm lay a long line of mountains, and we rode along the foot of the mountains to our farm, a distance of about three or four miles. Before we knew what was happening, bullets were whizzing all round us. There was a group of English on the farm, about fifty or sixty strong, shooting at us. We fled into the mountains and began defending ourselves. Of course the English didn't know how many of us there were, or whether there were other burghers behind. So they quickly left in the direction of Kruger station, and we went to ground in the kloof to wait for darkness.

I almost couldn't bear to look at our house like this—the yard was unkempt, and everything was growing wildly around the house; doors and windows had been broken out, and I couldn't help wondering what it must look like inside. I had a pressing desire to see the house, even just to gaze on the portraits of my dear parents who, for all I knew, might no longer be alive. Just to see once more where my mother had always sat doing needle-work, or where my father had knelt in prayer each evening.

My brothers and I decided to ride out to the house, but while we were still making our plans the order came to flee as the enemy was coming round the mountain. Again I had to tear myself away from the place that for me was almost sacred, and flee. We reached the foot of the mountain and gave our horses free rein. It was terrible, riding over fences and ditches with bullets whizzing around us. Luckily it was already dark, and we were soon out of danger.

Near the railway line the farms were not as badly destroyed—there were still some chickens, and in places even a pig to be seen. At one farm we found about fifty eggs and in the middle of them a hen sitting brooding, and every day the other hens came to lay more eggs. Probably no chickens ever hatched because each time the hens returned, they would sit on different eggs.

In one place we came across a flock of about two thousand sheep. The English had chased them into a patch of high grass, set the grass on fire, and encircled them to ensure that none escaped the fire. These animals were a terrible sight to see. Those not burnt to death had legs deformed by the heat, and were crawling about on their knees. Some of their eyeballs had burst, while others' lips had curled back over their teeth. Had I not seen it myself, I would never have believed that people existed who were capable of such cruelty. But these people would probably have done anything to starve out the Boers.

We headed for Philippolis, where we were due to meet the rest of the commando; and arrived safely after trekking through the night. The others were astonished to see us, for they'd heard we'd all been captured.

The same day we received word from the main laager that we should spend the coming Sunday quietly, as it was the day of humiliation and prayer for our women in the camps, as well as for the prisoners of war. That day we were on a farm in the district of Fauresmith. The laager was situated between two big, flat ridges overgrown with bushes; and there sat a large crowd of men, heads bowed, listening to the words of Oom Hendrik Strauss. He read Psalm 83. When I looked at the crowd—some no longer had hats, but only a piece of material tied over their heads; others had khaki blankets around themselves instead of jackets; many had springbok skin trousers; most were barefoot; a few had only a piece of ox-hide tied to their feet with thongs—I couldn't help myself. My heart was bursting with emotion, and I had to weep.

It was terrible to hear big, strong men crying like children. Will England ever be able to compensate our people for all our suffering, and all we had to go through in our fight for freedom? We erected a cairn in memory of the day we spent there. It stands to this day.

The whole commando stayed together, and our only hope was that the war wouldn't continue much longer, for we were in a shocking state. I had packed my clothes in trunks and hidden them here and there in the ridges—obviously I couldn't move around with lots of clothes—and I took with me only those I needed most. I had more than enough clothes, but it was often difficult to get hold of them. As we'd hidden some of our clothes at Boomplaas, and were passing close by, we decided we'd go and collect some of them before moving on in the direction of the Orange River.

I told my brothers that I didn't feel the least bit like going there, for, as I've already said, I had an awful fear of the place. They persuaded me, and I made them promise that they wouldn't leave me alone if I were captured. Well, we went to Boomplaas and found everything in good order there. We decided to spend the night, but outside the house for safety reasons. When the sun rose the following morning, we started preparing to return to the laager. *En route* a few more burghers joined us, and we were about ten riders in all. They told us there had been a battle here between the English and the Boers the previous day, and that they felt ill at ease.

After passing the first farm we rode in the direction of a ridge. Between the houses and the ridge was a fairly deep, dry ditch we had to ride through. When we reached the wall of the ditch, a group of Khakis jumped out, and the next thing I knew there were about five or six Tommies surrounding each burgher. They pulled the burghers from their horses, removed their bandoliers, and took their rifles. Then I noticed a couple walking towards me. They wanted to help me off my horse, but I told them to keep their filthy hands away from me, dismounted myself, and walked to my brothers. The English told me to hand over my weapon, but they didn't dare take it from me themselves. I took my rifle by the barrel and smashed the butt on a rock before handing it over to them. If they only knew how humiliated I felt at being captured, they'd have known that capture itself was punishment enough for me.

They took us to their main column which was stationed at Swartkoppies. I had no idea until that day how eager they'd been to capture me, for when we arrived at the column they shouted, 'Caught at last!' and threw their hats in the air. There I discovered that two men who'd been with our commando had gone over and joined the English, and they'd told the English all about me, including the fact that I had money on me.

The ten prisoners of war were then shackled together in pairs, and marched to the local prison in town. The English were eager to talk to me, but I was as cheeky as possible, for I knew they were going to punish me regardless of the way I behaved towards them —so I preferred to behave badly. I had no idea where they'd taken my brothers, only that we were now separated. They put me in a tent just behind that of the Commandant. What his name was I don't know. One doesn't hear people's names in such circumstances.

We remained there that night, and moved on the following

morning. Everything on the way was destroyed, fences were cut and trampled. The prisoners were chased on foot, and what made me really angry was the way the Africans, the Hottentots and the 'joiners' mocked the Boers. If the Boers walked too slowly, they would ride so close behind them that their horses' hooves cut the prisoners' heels. And the Boers couldn't go faster. They were absolutely exhausted. I felt as if I would die of rage. I despised the 'joiners' and forbade them to speak even one word to me. Their work was so low they couldn't have sunk lower. It was a bitter experience for me to see the prisoners walking like that, exhausted and finished, without a single opportunity to speak to them. The only time I got close to them was in the late afternoon, when the column halted to rest the animals.

It is not possible to appreciate how cruelly the English treated both humans and animals unless you saw and experienced it yourself. For example, when we encountered a flock of sheep, the poor animals were all chased into one kraal, and then two Englishmen caught them, while two others slit their throats. But not properly, so that the animal was dead. No, they just cut the main artery, threw the animals to one side, and left them there to bleed to death. We came across a sow with one shoulder amputated. When we found her she was already dead, but her ten little piglets were still suckling from their dead mother. I simply cannot describe everything my eyes encountered.

As I've already said, the two burghers who'd left us and joined the English had told them I was carrying money in my clothes. That was accurate enough, for while they were still with us, I'd had the money hidden in the hem of my dress, but because it sometimes got wet in the rain I'd taken it out, worked it into a piece of strong tarpaulin which I crafted into an envelope, and put the envelope in the front of my dress. It was not long before two nurses came to examine me. I argued until I was blue in the face that I had no money, but they told me to get undressed as they were certain I had money hidden somewhere in my clothes. First they felt the entire hem of my dress, then they wanted to see my underwear. I knelt down. Luckily I had the envelope against my skin, and when I undid my underwear, I moved the envelope as well, and allowed it to slide down with the clothes that ended up around my legs. My heart was beating so hard I felt certain they could hear it, and to distract them I said, 'Now do you see how the "joiners" lie?' They left the tent then, but it was a good few minutes before I could breathe normally once more.

It was getting late, and I saw the prisoners walking towards me. They passed close by my tent. The English planned it that way, because they knew how bitterly it would hurt me to see them like that. They were still shackled together in pairs. The English had forbidden us to talk to each other, but we couldn't go on like this. We had to make a plan to communicate with each other. I had so much to tell them about all the things I'd heard in the camp. So I started singing. The nurses watched me carefully, as did the Tommies, but what did they know about Afrikaans songs? In this way I told the burghers all I'd heard. At times it was difficult, for I couldn't always synchronise my words with the tunes. One of the officers asked me what I was singing, and I said it was a very popular war song. I knew he was making fun of me, but he couldn't regard me as a bigger fool than I regarded him, only I dared not say so.

Then the English caught sight of a Boer commando. They were afraid the Boers might free us, so they fled with us to Edenburg. From there we would probably be sent away. When we were half an hour's ride from the town, the column halted and set up camp. I knew I was going to be separated from my brothers, and I wanted to speak to them. I got permission to do so, and my youngest brother came over to me. He climbed into the cart with me, and asked, 'Sarah, where are you going?' I said I thought I was going to mother in the camp. I didn't wish to upset him unnecessarily, especially as he looked as though he might collapse at any moment. He was as white as a ghost, his eyes were sunken, and he was painfully thin.

Before he could say more, however, an Englishman arrived and pulled him off the cart, shouting, 'What are you talking about, you Dutch bastard? Get out!' The Englishman then used the butt of his rifle to hit my brother in the back, so hard that he fell over. The Englishman pulled him up again, and chased him back to the others.

I was ready to commit murder; and if my eyes had been cannons, not a single Englishman would have survived that day.

It was now dusk and it began to rain. Suddenly I heard the order, 'March the prisoners on!' My heart almost failed me, as I couldn't imagine what was going to happen now. I was standing between two guards, and it was so dark I could barely see twenty feet in front of me. The prisoners passed right in front of me, still shackled together in pairs. I started walking with them, for after all I was also a prisoner, but the guard shoved me back with his rifle saying, 'You stop here!'

He went and spoke to an officer. I waited in a state of great anxiety as it was pitch dark and I couldn't hear the other prisoners. My courage almost failed me, but I'd resolved that no Englishman would ever witness a tear of mine, so I did my best not to let them see how afraid I was.

After a while someone approached on horseback, and called out, 'Where are you?'

I gave no reply.

He shouted, 'Where is that damned lady prisoner?'

One of my guards answered that I was right in front of him, and he then said to me, 'March on!' So I walked along the road to Edenburg. It was so dark I could barely make out the road. I was cold, for an icy wind was blowing and my clothes were wet. The Englishman continually shone his torch on me, and if I disappeared from the beam for so much as an instant, he would shout, 'Where are you? I'll shoot!' I was entirely indifferent to this threat.

So things continued until we reached a swiftly running river. He shone his torch on the water, and ordered me to walk on. I entered the water, which came up to my knees, and he rode his horse behind me. When we reached the other side he asked me whether I was wet. I told him that that was a really stupid question, and that I was just as dry as he was. I walked on. Then I heard people talking, and when I got closer I saw it was my brothers and the other prisoners on their way to the camp. The officer then said, 'The lady may halt and say goodnight to her friends.'

The first thing they asked me was where I was being taken, and what they were going to do with me. In order to comfort them, I told them I was going to mother. I didn't even know if they heard my reply, for suddenly the English guards were driving them on again. I couldn't say anything further just then— I was afraid the English would hear my voice break with emotion. Those few minutes were indescribable for me. I almost broke down. I'd always been with my brothers, but now these ties too were being severed, so I had to summon all my courage and prepare myself for prison.

I walked to the Commandant's office. I knew every stone and every house in this town, and each one brought back sweet memories of the past, of this place where I'd spent my first school years. When I arrived at the office, I saw it was already eleven o'clock. There was a whole group of Englishmen sitting around. One asked me if I knew people in the town, and I replied that I knew everyone. He asked if I knew a certain person, and I answered that I knew him well. Then he ordered a guard to take me to the person concerned, and to ask him to put me up for the night. They would decide what to do with me the next day.

So I accompanied two of the guards to this person's house. I was very glad it was so dark, as it was humiliating to walk as a prisoner between two English guards through streets where everyone knew me. We arrived at the house, knocked, and heard someone coming to the front door. How happy I would be if I could spend just this one night under the roof of an old friend who knew me well, who had known my father for many years, and who had gone through many trials and tribulations with him. How happy my parents would be if they could know I was spending the night with him.

When the door opened and I saw his face, all hope deserted me. The guard asked him if he knew me. He looked at me and said, 'Evening, Sarah.' Nothing more. I told him the Commandant had sent me to ask if I could stay for the night, and that he had said they would decide what to do with me the next day. He remained quiet for a while, then he said, 'I will see,' and walked back into the house. I thought to myself that as he hadn't even asked me in, there was no doubt what his answer would be. When he returned, he said he was very sorry, but his wife was not well, and they didn't have room for me.

So I said, 'Good, thank you sir. I can see that you do not know me this evening, and as a result cannot offer me a place to stay for just one night,' and I walked with the guards back to the Commandant's office. The same thing happened at the second house we tried. This house was also too full to take me in for a single night.

Of course, they were too afraid to show me any friendship, for what would the English think if they were friendly towards a girl who'd been captured on the veld? Oh, if only they'd known what a terrible state I was in that night, how my soul longed for compassion, for a friendly look, for some comfort and encouragement in my bitter plight. That night I'd been separated from my two brothers, my only remaining pillars of support; and I was cold, wet, hungry and sick. I almost questioned the existence of God, and found myself on the brink of despair.

The Commandant himself was surprised when we returned a second time. I no longer cared what happened to me, and asked him why he didn't send me to my brothers in prison. After all I was also a prisoner, it was twelve o'clock at night, and I was not prepared to be dragged around from one house to the next only to be insulted. I told him I'd walked for half an hour in front of a horse to get there, that my clothes were beginning to dry on my body, that I was tired and wanted rest, and that he must please send me to prison.

He stood up, and after calling to somebody, said to me, 'Oh, you need not be in a hurry, you will get your punishment!'

SIX

When the person the Commandant had called arrived, he told him to bring the handcuffs. They were brought, and I was handcuffed. I then said to them that if they wished me to spend the whole night here, they must bring me dry clothes and also some food, as I was feeling faint. They paid no attention to me, except to say, 'Ask the Boers for food and clothing.'

After a while they asked me whether I knew Mrs Herbst, and when I answered yes, we headed for her house. There was a host of officers staying there, and also Boers who had joined the English. She had a boarding house. Some Afrikaners, like these 'joiners,' were not stupid. They went in under English protection, and so had experienced little of the war and had retained all their possessions. I was the foolish one to suffer like this; and yet, if I had to choose again, I've no doubt I would walk the same path. It was my passion to stand by my people, and to do so with a clear conscience. If I'd sided with the English, I'd never have been able to look an Afrikaner in the eye again. Indeed, those who did so *were* ashamed—they *were* unable to look one in the eye.

When Mrs Herbst opened her door, the guard asked her whether she knew me. She threw her arms around me, and insisted that I come into the house. When the guard told her I was a prisoner, and said that if she would take me in they would remove my handcuffs, and place a guard outside the house until the time came for me to go, she agreed and we entered the house. Inside was her mother, whom I met for the first time.

Later on Mrs Herbst took me to my room. I could see that she wanted to talk, as she was pacing about the room. I could hold out no longer, and had to give vent to my feelings, for it felt as if my heart was about to burst. I sat on the bed, and broke down in heartfelt tears. I asked her to please forgive me, but I had to give way to tears or I would die. She sat and cried with me for a long while; and when we eventually composed ourselves, she also decided it was time for bed.

After I'd removed my shoes and hung up my clothes, which by now were almost dry, I lay down. Every part of my body was stiff and sore, and although I lay on a bed—which was entirely strange to me, for I'd almost forgotten what a bed was like—I was unable to sleep. I was too tired, and just when I was on the verge of succumbing, I would see my two brothers handcuffed together, one wounded and the younger one as I'd last seen him, absolutely finished after the long march in the burning sun with blood streaming from his nose. And *ag*! he was still so young, and he never was a strong child.

Once when I'd just dropped off to sleep, I got such a fright that I jerked on the bed. In my dream, they were once more capturing me. I could hear the roar of the cannons, and I was trying to flee. By now I was fully awake, and the sorrow was breaking my heart. There was nobody to see me, and I prayed and wept bitterly, and eventually fell asleep.

Next morning I was woken by a knock on my door. When I answered, a voice outside said that people from the Commandant were here to talk to me. I got up and dressed slowly, for I knew all about the Commandant. I had after all got to know him the previous evening, and knew what to expect from him. In fact, it was strange to me that they didn't come and hurry me up, for I really did take my time getting dressed. When I eventually emerged, I saw two officers sitting on their horses. They jumped down as soon as they saw me. One came up to me and said the Commandant had asked them to take a photograph of me. I was instantly incensed. Imagine, after the treatment I'd received the day before, the cheek of wanting to take a photograph of me! It was of course just to be able to show they'd captured me.

I said to the officer as calmly as I could, 'You tell your Commandant that if one day I allow my photograph to be taken under better circumstances, he can buy one if he is so keen to have it,' and I walked back into the house.

Not long afterwards, one of the officers was back with the message that the Commandant wanted to see me at his office at nine o'clock. I quickly had something to eat, and the guard then escorted me to the Commandant's office. I was convinced in my own mind that I was on my way to gaol. But I discovered that they wanted to interrogate me about the Boers.

There were a number of Englishmen present, more than the previous evening. On the Commandant's desk stood a few pictures, one of General Hertzog, and two others I didn't recognise. The Commandant pointed at the photographs, and asked me whether I recognised them.

I answered, 'Extremely well.'

'Who are they?'

'Why do you want to know?'

'Because I want to know who they are.'

I said to him, 'It is sufficient for me to know. You can find out for yourself.'

Then he became extremely angry, and said to me, 'Do you know you are my prisoner, and that I can punish you?'

'You've no right to do that. I've worked for the Red Cross, and the very least I'm entitled to expect is civilised treatment,' I answered.

'What!' he cried. 'You who escaped from the Springfontein camp, and were recaptured under arms!'

He calmed down a little, and said, 'Look here, if you tell us now how you lived on commando, how strong you were, and how you blew up the railway line, I'll send you to your mother.'

I asked him if he knew where my mother was, and he said he didn't know, but that he would find out.

I was eager to find out where my mother and the others were, but when I heard that he didn't know, I could see that it wouldn't do any good to reason further with him. So I said, 'Do you really think that just because I've been captured I would commit treason?'

'Well, then, you can sit here until you decide to talk!'

'Understand me, if I had to sit here for eternity, I still wouldn't talk!'

Then he said to me, 'Your impertinence will get you nowhere. There's nothing more you can do for the Boers now!'

'Wait,' I answered, 'we'll see whether I'm capable of doing anything more for the Boers. And anyway, it would be better for me to be in gaol than to sit here any longer and look at your face. And when I'm free, I'll write and tell how so-called Great Britain's officers treated a weak and helpless girl.'

After this they rose and went into one of the other rooms. An interval passed, then the Commandant returned and asked if I was now ready to tell him what I knew about the Boers. I told him it was unnecessary to repeat the question, as I'd already told him I wouldn't say a word.

'Fine,' he answered, 'I'm now going to send you to gaol in Bloemfontein,' to which I replied that I was ready to leave.

The guard took me back to Mrs Herbst's house. I told her what had happened, and she warned me, '*Ag*, my child, you should have kept quiet. They'll punish you severely for being so cheeky.'

72

But again I thought to myself, Why should I keep quiet? They said whatever they liked to me; yet I wouldn't wish to speak of the treatment I got from most of them. If they'd treated me better, I'd have shown them I'd had a good upbringing, but under these circumstances I didn't consider it necessary.

I stayed with Mrs Herbst for seven days instead of leaving for Bloemfontein the next day as I'd expected. I was told to report to the Commandant's office every morning, but said I wouldn't— my guard could report there himself. The officers who were staying with Mrs Herbst always tried to talk to me, but I saw to it that they didn't get the chance, for I knew they only wanted to find out about the Boers.

One morning I was ordered to be at the Commandant's office at a particular time. One of the officers staying with Mrs Herbst came and walked with me. He began to talk to me, and asked whether I was feeling better. 'Yes, thank you,' I replied.

'Wouldn't you rather return to the veld?' he asked after a while.

'No,' I answered. 'Now that my brothers are captured, I don't wish to return.'

'What did you actually do in the veld?'

'Oh, nothing special. We just killed English, or captured them and "shook them out"!' I replied.

'And you told us you were in the Red Cross!' he exclaimed.

'And you keep telling me I was captured under arms,' I said.

'But wasn't that so?' he asked.

'I wonder.' Luckily we'd arrived at the office, and he wasn't able to continue the conversation.

On the seventh day they came and said I had to be ready to leave for Bloemfontein at twelve o'clock. Mrs Herbst quickly packed a few necessities for me, and at twelve on the dot two armed soldiers arrived to take me to the station. I took my leave of the people who'd received me so warmly.

Now I had to walk between the two soldiers to the station. I felt angry enough to overwhelm them both. When we arrived at the station, there was a whole group of people who had come to see me. I pretended I hadn't noticed them, but I saw very well who they all were, for I knew most of them. I thought to myself what a bunch of cowards they were, sheltering behind the blood of their own people. They were afraid that if they stood by their people they would lose their positions. Imagine, too ashamed to stand up and be counted for your own people! They would rather sit safely here and enrich themselves, while the rest of us suffered and strove for the cause. And then to come and look at me, as if I should be ashamed because I'd fought and, in my own simple way, done my best!

When after a while the train arrived, they moved a group of Africans out of one of the third class compartments, and told me to climb in with one of the guards. When the train left I opened the windows as the smell in the compartment was terrible. It didn't seem to bother the guard, who even asked me why I wanted to open all the windows. I told him it was because I had a nose that could smell.

The guard sat on the seat opposite me with his rifle next to him. I didn't say a word to him, I just sat and looked out the window. After a while it seemed strange to me that he was sitting so still; and when I looked, I saw he was fast asleep. I lent forward slowly, grabbed the rifle out of his hand, then went and stood in the doorway of the compartment and took aim at him. I shouted, 'Hands up!'

The Englishman jumped to his feet, both hands in the air, and pleaded for his life. Of course there was nothing I could do—I was on the train, and where could I escape to now? So I gave the rifle back to him, and he begged me not to tell anyone he'd fallen asleep. He also said he'd been ordered to shoot me if I tried to escape, but that he'd never have done it. If I wished to escape he would do nothing to stop me, I just mustn't tell anyone he'd fallen asleep.

But where could I escape to now? My brothers were captured, and I preferred to go through with what lay ahead of me. Maybe I would be reunited with my parents in the end.

When the train stopped at Bloemfontein station, there was once more a crowd of people to see me. I was ordered to disembark, and the guard followed me. There were so many spectators I had difficulty getting through them. Some wanted to talk to me, but the guard moved them away with his rifle. I held my head high, and pretended I saw and felt nothing, but I was full of turmoil inside. I was at once angry, heartsore, and shy—a real tangle of emotions. I heard someone saying, 'I wonder what they'll do with her, the poor thing, she looks so worn out and pale. Where is her mother? I truly pity her.' The word 'pity' upset me completely. I was so used to being handled roughly that the slightest sign of sympathy really affected me. I tried to get through the crowd as quickly as possible, as I didn't want them to see I had tears in my eyes.

I walked with the guard through the main street, Maitland Street, to the Commandant's office. When I entered, I found several officers as well as some of the so-called prominent citizens of Bloemfontein (Afrikaners) sitting there, and they all looked up when I came in. As usual they questioned me, which only made my burden heavier, for when interrogated I couldn't help insulting them, and they hated me the more for it.

The guard was ordered to take me to the boarding house of a certain Mrs Zoutendyk. There I was to be kept under surveillance once more. I was taken to my room, but, as I was taking off my hat, someone knocked on the door. There stood Dr Otto Krause, an old acquaintance and good friend of my father. He didn't give me a chance to speak. He didn't even greet me. I heard him say, 'I've come to fetch you. I was at the station. I know everything.

I was among the group that followed you to the Commandant's office.'

When I was able to speak, I said, 'But, Doctor, there are guards surrounding the house. How will I ever get away from here?'

'Nonsense!' he said. 'I saw the Commandant and he gave permission for you to come and stay with us. The guards will keep you under surveillance there instead of here.'

I was so happy I almost couldn't thank him, and while I was still trying to find words, he said, 'You must come with me immediately.'

What a warm and friendly reception I received from Mrs Krause! Only then did I truly learn what real friendship means in a time of sorrow and need. It felt as if I were back in my parents' home. The English could stand guard outside, but within those four walls I felt free. I could speak from the heart to people who understood only too well, for had they not struggled and suffered themselves? Dr Krause had himself been thrown in gaol on a cold cement floor. When he'd been captured, he was put on the train with a coop full of chickens, and he said the chicken lice almost ate him alive. I wished I could have stayed with the Doctor until the war was over.

It was a Sunday when I was taken to them, and from then on I appeared daily in front of a court martial. They interrogated me repeatedly about how the Boers lived, how much food they still had, how long I thought they could hold out, how they blew up the railway line, and so on. Every morning when the guard came to fetch me, Dr Krause advised, 'Tell them nothing. Say nothing. They can't punish you for that.'

One day the guard told me he had a letter for me from the Commandant which I had to take to another building a bit further up the street. This was now really a case of from Herod to Caiafas, from Caiafas to Pilot, and the end would surely also be death. When we arrived, I recognised a certain Mr Abram X, dressed in khaki and with his legs bound. Astonished, I asked what he was doing here, but he didn't answer and simply motioned to the door I had to enter.

When the guard opened the door for me, I saw there was only one person inside. I gave him the letter from the Commandant which the guard had handed me at the door.

After he'd read the letter, he looked up and said, 'Miss Raal, according to this letter, you are the lady who fought.' Naturally he was speaking English. I wondered what was afoot now. He spoke again, 'According to the letter I'm to interrogate you about your life on the veld. Are you willing to answer?'

I said to him, 'I've nothing to say. And if you mean to punish me because I won't betray my own people, you might as well begin. I'm ready.'

He looked at me compassionately, and said, 'Look, I will give you good advice, as a friend. Understand me well, as a friend.'

I was so taken aback to hear this kind of talk that I could hardly believe my ears, and my first thought was that this must be a cunning ploy. But the man had such a pleasant and open face I wasn't sure what to make of him. He continued, and then I could see he was being frank with me, for he said, 'They cannot punish you if you don't wish to speak. But as you are now in their hands, just keep very quiet. Personally, I admire your courage, but I'm not supposed to say such things to you. Where are you staying?'

'With Dr Otto Krause,' I said.

'Fine, I will come and look you up there.'

'How will you be able to come? There are guards surrounding the house. Surely they will see you,' I said.

'That doesn't matter. Wait a minute, I'm going to write a letter to the Commandant, and you can take it with you.'

While he was writing, I again sat and wondered whether he

77

was really being honest, or whether he was just being devious. But I'd learned not to make trouble unnecessarily.

After I received the letter from him, I returned with the guard to the Commandant's office, where I handed over the letter. After the Commandant had read it, he told the guard to return me to Dr Krause's house.

On the Saturday night, my English friend came to visit me. I was still uneasy, and chose my words carefully.

He told me they would no longer interrogate me, and added, 'I understand they are going to send you away from Bloemfontein.'

'Where to?' I asked.

'I'm not sure, but I believe to a concentration camp,' he said.

'Why can't I stay here in Bloemfontein where my mother is?' I wanted to know, for at that stage I had no idea that my mother had long been in the camp at Bethulie.

He shrugged his shoulders and said I must be ready to leave at any time. When he rose to leave, he gave me his address and added, 'Let me know what happens to you, and if things don't go well, at least you'll know where a friend is who greatly admires your courage.'

Then I said to him, 'How will I be able to write to you? All letters are censored—a letter from me would never reach you.'

'Oh, no,' he said, 'my post doesn't get read. The letter will be safe.'

Then he left.

I went and told Dr and Mrs Krause everything, also that I had to be ready to leave at any time. After the Doctor had taken it all in, he said he would immediately pack some medicines for me, and that he would label each bottle with what it was for. 'Because,' he said, 'you will surely need it.' Mrs Krause also inquired what I needed and what she could do for me.

My heart ached at the thought that I would have to leave this

78

house and these beloved friends. It bothered me terribly that I'd still not told them about the money I had on me. If I were now to die in a camp, what would happen to the money? At times I'd thought I should tell them, but then I'd reconsidered. Yet, if I was to tell anyone the secret I'd preserved for so long, now was the best opportunity I was likely to get.

SEVEN

Mrs Krause and I walked to my bedroom to see if there was anything I might need which she could give me. Once we were in the room I told her I needed to speak to her. By then I was in such a state of agitation I could speak no longer, and I burst into tears. Mrs Krause stood up, locked the door, came over to me, hugged me to her, and cried with me, saying, 'Feel free to speak, my child; treat me as your mother, and tell me what is worrying you.'

I got straight to the point and said, 'Do you know, Mrs Krause, I have £500 that I've kept on me all the time I've been on commando. I've carried it on my chest all this time.'

She was dumbfounded, and wanted to know how I'd managed to survive wind, weather and commando life with the money intact. I told her that when my mother was taken captive I was stuck with the money and had no idea what to do with it, so I sewed it into the hem of my dress. I'd given £300 in notes to Commandant Fourie, who gave me 'Blue Backs' in exchange, as proof, and I'd worked this proof and the other money into the band on my hat.

Mrs Krause wanted to know where the dress and the hat were now. I told her they'd probably long since fallen to pieces, and that this was why I now had to carry the money in my clothes on my chest. I showed her the money and the proof I'd got, and also the receipt given to me by the enemy the first time I was captured. I also told her how difficult it had been on commando when it rained. When the dress had served its purpose and was no longer wearable, I'd had to make another plan. So I took all the money and the receipts and worked them into a piece of strong tarpaulin which I'd crafted into an envelope. I could still hear the few burghers who knew about the money saying to me when it was raining, and I was struggling to dry the money, 'You might as well give up the money. You'll never get through the war with it. And if the Khakis catch you, they'll only use it to oppress us further.'

After I'd told her everything, Mrs Krause kept asking me how she could help, and what we could do.

I then asked her for a pillow and said that if I got sick in the camp, I'd ask somebody with whom I was friends—for I would surely make some friends in the camp—to send the pillow to the address I would leave on it. What I meant was, in case I died. Then Mrs Krause would be able to give the money hidden in the pillow to my parents if they were still alive.

'But,' she argued, 'will you be able to find someone you can trust?'

'Mrs Krause,' I replied, 'I wouldn't tell them there was money in the pillow. I'd just ask them to send it to you if I should die.'

Finally she agreed, and undertook that if ever she received the pillow she would send the money to my parents or other family.

It was almost twelve o'clock, and I knew I should rest to gather as much strength as possible for the next day, when my new life would begin.

I went to bed with a much lighter heart than usual, but getting to sleep remained a lost cause. I was so afraid of the morrow. If only I could be back on commando, surrounded by the beauty of nature and breathing fresh air, how happy and free I'd feel. I fell asleep at about three o'clock, only to be woken almost immediately by terrible dreams that left my heart racing.

Next morning I woke with a start when the breakfast bell rang. I dressed quickly and went to the dinning room, but I could neither eat nor talk. Dr Krause asked me what the matter was, and when I looked up I saw that Mrs Krause's eyes were moist with tears. That was it. I stood up and went to my room, Mrs Krause joined me, and we cried together again. I told her I thought it would be better if they came and fetched me right away. The uncertainty was just too much. I knew I couldn't stay where I was, and I wanted to get it over and done with, whatever lay ahead.

There was a knock on the door, and Dr Krause came in. He looked at me and asked whether I was feeling unwell, and why I was so pale. I told him I wasn't sick, just downcast. He said I had to go with him because two Englishmen had come to fetch me. I fetched my things, and after saying a bitter farewell to those two dear people, I left with the guards.

We arrived at the station at about half-past eight, and I sat down on a bench to wait for the train. As it was Sunday the station was quiet, and I sat whiling the hours away. By twelve o'clock I'd developed a terrible headache. I was tired from not getting enough sleep the previous night, and hungry. Why couldn't they let me stay with Dr Krause until later? I had to sit endlessly with a guard at my side. Once I had to warn him to keep his distance unless he wanted a good *klap* from me, and he didn't try coming too close again.

I waited and waited, but there was no sign of any train. Three o'clock came, four o'clock ... by nine o'clock that evening I was still sitting there without a morsel of food or a drop of water having passed my lips. The warm westerly wind we Free Staters knew so well blew me half to death, and my whole body was full of aches and pains from sitting on the hard bench all day. They wouldn't let me into the waiting room. English people at the station kept walking in my direction and looking at me, as if they wished to talk to me, but I pretended to be reading and held up a book in front of my face. After a while I started feeling really sick with hunger, but there was nobody to talk to. I didn't wish to exchange a single word with the detestable Khaki. I thought they must be trying to starve me to death! After all, they wanted to get rid of me, and it wouldn't look so bad that way. They couldn't shoot me in cold blood, although in certain circumstances that might indeed have been preferable.

I saw someone walking towards me. He seemed to be looking for somebody. Then I noticed that it was my English friend, Captain Reed. When he saw me, he came directly over. He asked how long I'd been at the station, and when I told him since nine o'clock that morning, he almost fell on his back. He asked if I'd had anything to eat, and I answered that not even a drop of water had passed my lips. When he asked why I was still sitting there, and why I'd had nothing to eat, I replied, 'That you must ask your Commandant, and when you do tell him that Miss Raal says he is the most barbaric monster in all creation!'

He stepped closer and spoke to me softly, 'Please, Miss Raal, rather keep quiet or the guard will report you.'

While we were still talking, the long awaited train entered the station. I was told that we would have to spend the night on the train, and that it wouldn't leave Bloemfontein until the following morning as they were worried the railway line might be blown up. In the meanwhile I found out from Captain Reed that I was being sent to the Kroonstad camp, although he wasn't entirely certain of this. When the train stopped, the compartment directly in front of us had two English nurses in it. Captain Reed walked up to the carriage, and after talking to the nurses he returned and said I should come and have a cup of tea. At first I wanted to refuse, but I felt so nauseous with hunger that I went along. He took me to the two nurses but did not get into the train, and went and stood a little way away. The nurses gave me a cup of tea and a buttered roll. After I'd eaten we started talking, and one of the nurses asked, 'How far are you going?'

My answer, 'I really don't know, I'm a prisoner' had the same effect as if someone had ignited a stick of dynamite in the compartment. They called the captain, and even before he arrived they told me to get out, and said I couldn't stay there. I thanked them for the tea and got out. The guard was already waiting for me, and he took me back to the bench. My English friend returned, and sat down next to me. He told the guard to go, and said he'd call him when he should return. I could tell that his friendship was true, and that he genuinely empathised with me.

After the guard had left Captain Reed said to me, 'Look, I'd like to give you something. You mustn't take it as an insult. It's given purely out of sympathy and fellow suffering, and I wish I could do more, but that doesn't lie within my power.'

He took a wallet out of his pocket and said, 'Please, take this from me as proof of someone who sympathises deeply with you. You're bound to need it.'

I shook my head. 'Thank you, that's very kind of you. I accept that you do sympathise with me, but I can't take the money. There's nothing I need and, besides, the English have taken all my things, even the precious diary I wouldn't have traded for the world. They'd probably take the money as well.'

He told me I had his address, and that I should let him know what happened to me. Then he called the guard, and told him where I should get on to the train. After saying goodbye, he left.

I got into one of the compartments with the guard, who was armed, although I couldn't imagine why. I sat at an angle in one corner and he sat opposite me, straight as an ironing board, hand on rifle. I waited and waited for something to eat, but in vain. Every now and then someone would appear at the window to see what I looked like. I felt like somebody who'd been given the death sentence whom they were coming to see one last time. When I saw that it was getting very late and that I was not going to get anything to eat, I lay down on the bench. I didn't dare fall asleep because the Khaki was there right in front of me. Who knows, maybe he'd been given orders to shoot me in my sleep. One thing was sure, and that was that this soldier was going to get no sleep either. Whenever I saw him close his eyes, I would move about so he would know I was awake. Thus we spent the night.

We finally left at eight o'clock the next morning. At the first station we reached I was ordered off the train, and I'd barely got off when I was told to get back on again. So it went at every moderately sized station where we stopped. Eventually I asked the guard why I had to get off each time, and he said it was because they were taking photographs of me.

At the next station the guard again told me to get out, but no way was I going to do so. He told me I must. I replied that I was very sorry but that I most certainly would not. Then two other Englishmen arrived and told me to get out. That really got me going, and I said to them, 'You go to the devil,' slammed my window shut, and lay down on the bench. After that they left me in peace, but I felt terrible. My head was so sore I thought it would burst, and I was starving, but I'd rather have died of hunger than ask them for a drop of water.

We arrived in Kroonstad at two o'clock on the Monday afternoon. If only the English had treated me less harshly, things would have been better. But the reality was that if they as much as looked at me strangely, my blood would boil. However, I felt that in the circumstances it would be better for me not to get too upset. I might faint, and that I didn't want to do in front of the English.

When I got off the train I was once more taken directly to a court martial. Thankfully, it was not long before one of the

Englishmen told my guard that there was a cart outside waiting to take me to the camp. I cannot describe how pleased I was to hear that! However awful life in the camps might be, it had to be better than what I'd just gone through. They would surely have some food for me, and I would at last be able to rest.

Had I but known what lay in store for me, I'd probably have shot the Englishman dead on the train and tried to escape again. At the camp, the guard took me to Commandant Thomson. It was precisely four o'clock when we reached him. The guard gave him the blue piece of paper he'd brought with him from Bloemfontein, and I stood waiting while he read it. After a while he peered at me from under his wild eyebrows, and he motioned to a chair. I was grateful to be able to sit. He walked out of the office, returned later, and continued with his work. I wondered what he had in mind for me. I'd last eaten on Sunday morning, apart from the cup of tea and the buttered roll in Bloemfontein, and it was now almost five o'clock. Also, I'd not slept a wink the previous night. I could feel that my legs wouldn't be able to carry me very far, and my head was spinning. Eventually I said to him, 'What are you going to do with me? Do you know that I had my last meal on Sunday morning, and that I'm sick and hungry! Why don't you send me to the camp? I need rest.'

He sprang to his feet and said, 'You will never go to the Refugee Camp. You shall go to the Bird Cage, a good distance from here!'

By then I was really angry and didn't care what happened to me. So I said to him, 'Well, send me there, I am sure it will be better than looking at your face!'

With that he once again left the room. One of the others who stayed behind asked me why I was so cheeky, but before I could reply he returned. He looked at me with venom, and said sarcastically, 'You may go.' To the guard, he said, 'March her on.'

When we emerged from the tent I saw four Khaki-Boers dragging a tent past us. The guard took the small trunk I'd brought from Bloemfontein, and we followed the Khaki-Boers. I could see they were taking me in a completely different direction to the women's camp. It was almost dark owing to a terrible storm that was brewing. I asked one of the Khaki-Boers where they were taking me, and he said, 'You're going to the camp where we lock up troublemakers.'

I was too tired and sick to answer him back, and I was walking as fast as I could just to keep up, as a strong wind was blowing and the weather was threatening to break. One of them must have noticed me dragging my feet, for he said sarcastically, 'Hold out a little longer, you'll soon arrive where you can rest a long, long time.' They looked at each other and laughed.

Finally we arrived at my resting place. It was a camp, a hundred feet square, fenced with barbed wire. There wasn't even a gate, and the fence had to be lifted up so I could crawl under it. I could hardly stand, and I just prayed that God would help me not to faint in front of the English and the Khaki-Boers. They erected my tent in the middle of the camp, put my trunk inside it, and walked away. Four armed guards circled the camp.

I sat down on my trunk. I felt as if I'd reached the end of my life, or if not, that I'd probably have to stay here until the end of the war. But I realised that I couldn't allow myself to think about dying. What would become of my parents? If I could only get something to eat, I might feel better. It was pitch black outside, I'd had nothing to eat, and the threatening weather now broke into a wild storm. All I could see was lightening, there were heavy claps of thunder, and the sound of the raging wind buffeted my tentflaps. I felt as if death were stalking me, and I was unable to flee. The English had given me one rough blanket, but I also had the pillow and blanket Mrs Krause had given me. They were both still in the trunk. I felt for the key hanging round my neck on a piece of string, then for the keyhole of the trunk. I unlocked it, and took out the pillow and blanket. I would dearly have liked to take some of the medicine Dr Krause had given me, but it was too dark to read what was written on the bottles. I made a bed of sorts in the dark, and lay down. But I couldn't lie comfortably, and couldn't work out what was the matter. The ground was surely not too hard. Hadn't I slept on the ground every night for almost a year? It must have been because I'd slept on a comfortable bed at Mrs Krause's house for a while, and was now no longer used to sleeping on the ground. I sat up. I prayed that God, who had led me through so much danger, wouldn't desert me now. I couldn't even pray properly, my mind was now so dulled. I fell down on my knees. If only I could sleep, I wouldn't feel the hunger pangs so badly. But I could feel myself giving up hope. I was exhausted.

How long I lay there I cannot say. The next thing I became aware of was that water was running in one side of the tent and out the other, and that I was drenched. I pulled my trunk next to the tent pole and sat on top of it. I hadn't been sitting there long when the tent pole broke, and I fell under the wet tent. I crawled out so that only my head was free, and I held one side of the tent over me.

I don't know whether I fell asleep or whether I fainted. When I woke, the sun had been up for some time. I pulled out my trunk, threw open my blankets to dry, and changed into dry clothes. Then I sat on the trunk to see what the day would bring. Perhaps I would get some food. The guards were still keeping watch around the camp. The sun was shining beautifully after the terrible, stormy night. The dear earth looked fresh and clean. In the distance I could see the concentration camp. Everywhere there was smoke rising, and I could see people moving about and working. I wondered whether somewhere there was someone who would take pity on me.

Then I heard something behind me, and when I turned round I saw two of the guards walking towards me. They walked past me without saying a word, and went to pull my trunk back next to the tent pole. I called to them, and said, 'Look, I'm going to the camp now.' I stood up and started walking to the fence. One of them stopped me and asked what I wanted. I told him *food*, and walked on. 'Wait, stand still,' one of them commanded, 'we've been ordered to shoot you if you cause any trouble!'

I replied, 'Shoot if you must, but I'm going to get some food.' He blocked my path with his rifle, saying he would go and speak to the Commandant. He walked to the camp while the other three kept watch. Now I wanted to take some medicine, but my legs were too exhausted from the exertion of getting to the tent and, besides, I didn't have any water to take it with. So I sat and waited. I wondered whether I was becoming ill, or whether it was just the hunger and thirst that made me feel so terrible.

A 'Bird Cage' similar to that in which Sarah Raal
almost met her end.

EIGHT

After a while the guard returned with a tin of water, about ten klinkers (hard biscuits eaten by the troops), and half a tin of bully beef. He handed me the food, told me it was my rations for the day, then turned around and walked away. I called after him that he should tell the Commandant I was not a pig in a cage and that he must give me better food, or I would report him to the Boers when they arrived. The guard didn't answer me, he simply walked away.

I'm going to escape from this place, I thought to myself, but unless I ate right away I'd die of hunger instead. So I tasted the meat, which was like chewing on a crystal of salt. I tried the klinkers, but to eat them I would have to sacrifice my teeth. Yet I had to get something into my stomach, so I ate a little of the meat and drank some of the water. Then I had to rest, for I'd need all my energy to escape. I put some of the klinkers into the water to soften them.

I lay down and immediately fell asleep, but it wasn't long before I was once more plagued by terrible dreams, and after that I couldn't sleep at all. It felt as if I were losing my mind.

When I thought about the money my courage returned. I stood up, wanting to eat the klinkers I'd soaked in the water, but they were no softer. I drank the water, which was unpleasantly hot, but I was terribly thirsty; and before I knew it the water was finished.

The guard had told me these were my rations for the day, but water cost nothing—surely they would give me more water. I called one of the soldiers and asked him for more water, which he later brought. After eating some more meat, I lay down again and took out my pocket Bible. Then I fell asleep.

When I woke I felt a little better. There was nothing else to do, so I started unpacking my trunk to see what was inside, and to look through the medicines. The Doctor had packed medicines for fever, headache, stomach pains and so on, and Mrs Krause had packed writing paper, a clean pillow case, towels, two pairs of stockings, thread, and needles and pins. I so longed to be with them, but refused to let sadness get the better of me. So I quickly packed everything away and went out to inspect the camp, to assess the prospects for escape—where to I had no idea, as both my brothers were captured. I would also not be able to make any immediate attempt, for I could feel that there was something wrong with me. I had continual headache and fever, and could only take a few steps without becoming tired. And the bully beef left me with a constant thirst.

I found the nights unbearably long in my prison, and I didn't even have a candle. I never slept at night. I slept during the day. I was too afraid of the guards keeping watch outside to do so at night. I had nothing with which to protect myself if they bothered me. These were the things I lay and worried about through each long night. If only I could have some light, I would at least be able to read. More than once I thought of writing to my English friend and asking his advice. Then I felt ashamed for wanting to ask the enemy for help or mercy. I decided that if I had to die of hunger here, I would tear up the money rather than allow it to fall into enemy hands. I begged them for light, and eventually I paid a guard half a crown for a packet of candles—or I would still have been sitting in a dark tent. Should I ask the enemy for mercy now, possibly in my last hours? No, never! If I had to die, I would die an Afrikaner, faithful unto death.

So one day after another passed. If only I could have slept the time away, my illness wouldn't have troubled me, and I'd have had no time to think. But in this condition, I constantly relived recent events with vivid clarity, and shuddered to think of everything I'd experienced on commando. I saw again only too clearly how poor, dumb animals were murdered, and thousands of sheep were chased into a kraal and bayoneted to death. Some I saw were dead, others lay there bleeding to death. I saw the enemy chase a troop of horses into a kraal, then turn their cannons on them, and blow them to smithereens.

I tried to banish such thoughts, but to no avail. They churned around in my head, and I was literally too sick and too tired to fight them. I felt I was succumbing. Then I thought about things in the camp. There was just as much senseless murder going on in the camp. Here finely ground glass and vitriol were put into the sugar. One day I saw a young boy being carried to the morgue, and when they were half way there he said, 'Sir, where are you taking me now?'

Would God really allow our nation to be exterminated in this way? Surely the wheel would turn, and another nation would attack them and wipe out their youth! The time would come when they would suffer just as we, innocently, were suffering.

My stomach was so weakened by the salty meat that nothing would stay down. No sooner had I swallowed than I lost it again, and I could no longer even make it to my private toilet space. I was too weak to walk. In the evenings, when my light was out, I would crawl there on my hands and knees and sit for hours, sometimes until dawn. Then I would crawl back to my tent and lie there in a heap.

My pen will not write everything I endured. If the English intended me to go through hell, they certainly succeeded. I knew I was sick, and that my strength was fading. Finally, at the end of my tether, before I lay down, I took my pillow, cut open a corner, hid the money among the feathers, and sewed the pillow closed. Then I lifted my pen and wrote the following letter to the Commandant:

'Sir

This is the last request of a dying woman. May God give you grace to grant it. Please send the pillow on which I'll breath my last, to the address you will find on same.

Thank you

Sarah Raal'

I placed the letter on my trunk, then I collapsed in pain. My tongue was so dry and swollen I could hardly even pray. I just lay there waiting to die. The candle was still burning in front of me, and I heard someone say, as if from a great distance, 'Lights out!' Again I sank beneath a wave of pain. After a while I felt someone lifting my head, and when I opened my eyes I saw one of the guards on one knee next to me. He steadied his rifle with one hand while he lifted my head with the other. I heard him whisper softly, 'My God, why must you suffer so?' Then he stood up and left.

Not long after that they arrived to take me to hospital. When they lifted me on to the stretcher I kept hold of my pillow which they put under my head. They carried me quickly and we arrived at a big tent. Everything there looked unfamiliar, but by now I no longer cared. Fortunately I recognised the first sister who came up to me. She was Miss Wessels, and we'd been together in the Springfontein camp. I was so pleased to see her! All I said was, 'Sister, please let me lie on my own pillow,' and she replied, 'Of course, of course, don't talk, you're very ill.'

The doctor arrived and examined me. He called the nurse aside, and said to her, 'Sister, her temperature is very high and she has inflammation of the stomach. Keep her very quiet. I'll come back and see her later.' That was the last I heard. The world started spinning around me, and I must have lost consciousness.

When I came to I couldn't work out where I was. I lay there and gazed around me, but had no idea how I'd got to wherever I was. I became terribly afraid and wanted to flee, but couldn't move my body. Somebody came and held me on the bed. Then I lost consciousness again. A while later I came round, and this time Sister Wessels was beside me. I recognised her, but before I could open my mouth she said, 'Don't speak, my child, you've been at death's door. I'm thankful you've regained consciousness, but don't move or try to talk. You're by no means out of danger yet. Last night you were delirious and talked about all sorts of things. The doctor gave you an injection to make you sleep, and the rest has been good for you.'

Suddenly I remembered my pillow and wanted to check that it was still there, but I was too weak. Sister Wessels bent over me and whispered, 'I know what you're looking for. All is well. Your pillow is still under your head.' Against my will I started to cry, and although I tried I couldn't stop crying. Eventually Sister Wessels called the doctor. He said I must try and stop, as my body wouldn't be able to take it if I kept on crying. But try as I might, I just couldn't hold back the tears, and a little while later he gave me something to make me sleep. I immediately began to feel drowsy, and soon I fell into a long, deep sleep from which I woke a long while later.

Slowly I began to recover, but I was still extremely weak, and drank almost nothing but milk. I was in no hurry to leave, however, as my treatment in hospital was far better than anything I could expect in the 'Bird Cage'. I would try to stay where I was as long as possible, for who knew what they might do with me once I was discharged from hospital.

After a week they moved me to another part of the hospital to regain my strength. There I received many visitors, more out of curiosity than anything else. They said that they'd heard about the 'angry, brave girl' and that they'd come to see what I looked like. From as far afield as Kroonstad I received flowers and books, and even delicacies but these I wasn't yet able to eat, so I gave them to the other patients who, believe it or not, were envious of my lot.

More than one visitor asked what would happen to me once I was discharged from hospital. I answered that I had no idea, and that I really didn't care. They asked why I didn't go and apologise to the Commandant and ask him to send me to the women's camp. But I couldn't see why I should apologise. I'd done nothing wrong. It was rather his duty to come and apologise to me for the treatment I'd received from him.

One day one of the English nurses told me that the letter I'd written to the Commandant had had a wonderful effect on him. He himself had ordered milk for me from the town, and every day they'd had to report to him on my condition. But the English had so often almost got me into trouble with their compliments that I no longer believed a word I heard from them.

I recovered quickly, and one day Sister Wessels asked me whether I wouldn't like to become a nurse. I replied that I thought the life of a nurse would kill me faster than the 'Bird Cage'. I wouldn't be able to withstand people's suffering. 'What are you going to do then?' she wanted to know. I told her, 'Now then, sister, how can you ask me such a question? I have no say in the matter. Commandant Thomson will make that decision.' Then she told me that the nurses had gone to the Commandant and asked him not to send me back to the 'Bird Cage'. But I didn't mind if I was locked up in that cage again. I'd be quite happy if only they gave me better food and allowed me out from time to

95

time. Although I knew many people in the camp, I actually preferred being alone.

A week passed in this manner. Then one day, while I was sitting building castles in the air, who should come to visit me but Commandant Thomson himself. He asked if I was strong enough to leave the hospital, and I said that I was.

'Well then,' he continued, 'I'm going to send you to the camp. You'll share a tent with Miss Kidman, an English lady, but this arrangement is subject to one condition.' He remained silent for a moment, and I looked up to see why he'd stopped. He looked me in the eye and said, 'That is that you promise to go and live quietly, and not stir up trouble among the Boers here in the camp.'

'Okay, I will promise that,' I replied, 'but also subject to one condition. That is that you tell the Khaki-Boers to leave me alone and not to bother me, and also not to talk to me about the Boers in the veld.'

He agreed.

After this conversation with the Commandant I returned to my room, for as it was I'd already left my pillow unattended for far too long.

When I returned, everyone wanted to know what the Commandant had said. I told them everything, and they congratulated me for getting off so lightly. I asked what had happened to my trunk and blankets, and was told that they were safe, but that they would only be returned to me the following day. That evening when I went to bed, each of the nurses came to bid me farewell with a kiss.

The following morning Sister Wessels took me to her mother, and I spent the day there. Mrs Wessels offered to cook my food every day with hers, for which I was very grateful as I knew nothing about cooking in the camp. The food was pathetic enough to see, and I felt sure that if I'd had to cook and struggle for myself, I'd have died of hunger. I also slept over with Mrs Wessels, and when I got to my tent the following morning Miss Kidman was already there. Why they had to place this raw young Englishwoman in my tent with me I had no idea, but I had my suspicions. We would just have to come to terms with the situation. As long as she treated me well, I would show her that we Afrikaner girls were just as cultured as she was. But I was none too pleased about having to share with her.

That first afternoon in my own tent I walked through the entire camp, and had a good look at everything. I couldn't understand how people still had the courage to go on living. In almost every tent I could hear the groaning of the sick, and every day six or seven people were buried. Little children were wrenched from their mothers' breasts and taken to the hospital, from where they never returned. I also saw children who were still alive being taken to the morgue. In the hospital I saw little ones too weak to swat the flies away from their faces. The flies would crawl up their noses, and before long worms would be crawling out of their nostrils. I almost lost my mind amid all this suffering and torment.

There were between four and five thousand people in the camp, of whom many were 'National Scouts' who had to do all the dirty work in the camp, such as collecting wood and fixing tents. Every morning we had to collect our own rations. A large tarpaulin was spread on the ground, our names were called out one by one, and a piece of meat was thrown on to the tarpaulin for each of us!

My life wasn't altogether unbearable, but the one thing I found especially difficult was the fact that I'd had no news of my parents. I didn't even know if they were still alive. I'd written to the other camps since being in this one, but had heard nothing. It was the uncertainty that caused so much anxiety. If they were in one of the other camps, surely they'd have received my letter and replied? I comforted myself with the thought that my letters had perhaps never been sent. Mrs Wessels always gave me courage, and with her help I managed to survive, and to keep on living with hope.

It will never be possible to compensate the women for all the pain and suffering they endured in the camps. The strategies devised by mothers so that their children wouldn't be taken away to the hospital were innumerable. Every afternoon the doctor and a nurse would do their rounds to see if there were sick people in any of the tents. When someone was sick and it was time for the doctor's visit, the patient would quickly be dressed and when the doctor entered the tent the person concerned would be busily engaged in something, so that the doctor wouldn't suspect that anything was amiss. Perhaps he would be washing his face if he were a man, or she would be knitting if she were a woman, and they would continue until the inspection was over. After that they would return to bed.

Next to my tent was a certain Mrs van Zyl. She had an only child, a beautiful seventeen year old daughter. Her husband had died on commando, and a short while later her daughter had taken ill. Every time the doctor came on his rounds, she would sit up and do some needlework. In this way her mother took care of her until she started getting better. But a few 'joiners' had seen what was going on, and they reported it to the hospital. The same day they came to take her away. Her mother did not want to let the child go, and they had to use force to remove the child from her arms. She fell to her knees and prayed for mercy, begging them not to take her child, but to no avail. They took the girl to the hospital, and wouldn't allow her mother to visit because, they said, it wouldn't be good for the child to see anyone. Eight days after she was taken away they sent for the mother, and when she arrived the child died. She hadn't even been able to recognise her mother. Her eyes had given in. The mother lost her mind.

Can such a thing ever be forgotten? Every child in the camp was just skin and bone, with huge eyes sunk into the back of their heads, and all day they complained of hunger. Some days their mothers had to stand and wait until noon before their names were called out to fetch their ration of meat, and until then their children stood with pale faces, tugging at their skirts, begging for food.

I couldn't sit there all day watching the pain and suffering, but I didn't know what else to do. So I went and asked Commandant Thomson for permission to go to Kroonstad in the afternoons. He gave me a pass that enabled me to go every afternoon, but I had to be back by a specific time and report my presence on my return. As long as the Englishwoman was with me this wasn't really necessary, as she was good enough to walk with me, and saw to it that they knew everything that was going on. We got on well until she started entertaining English people in our tent. Then I went off to old Thomson and told him he must give me a tent of my own. Naturally he wanted to know why I wished to be alone, so I told him, 'Because I won't allow Miss Kidman to entertain English people in my tent.'

'But don't you receive Boers in your tent?' he wanted to know. I told him there were no Boers in the camp. He promised to investigate the matter.

A few days passed and Miss Kidman was still with me, but the visits from the English had stopped. Then one morning she told me she was leaving. I was so happy I could have shouted out loud. My friends told me that, cheeky as I was, I was obviously in old Thomson's good books. However, I replied that I'd asked for no favours, and that they were obliged to take care of me.

By this time I'd been in the camp for six months, and still I'd had no news of my parents. Then one day I got word that they were in the camp at Bethulie, and I went straight to Thomson and asked him to send me to my parents. He told me that many of those who'd been at Bethulie had been moved to Uitenhage, and that he would try to find out where my parents were. He also told me that I would need the consent of the Provost Marshal, and that I would have to call on him in Kroonstad.

Next morning I set off for Kroonstad, but before I went to the office I dropped in on Mrs Andries Wessels as I knew her well, and had previously met the Provost Marshal at her house. I must admit that he had on that occasion been very friendly to me. As I turned the corner I saw that, sure enough, there he was sitting with her on the stoep. I went to the house, and came straight to the point. I told him I'd come to town that day specially to see him. The old man stood up and said, 'All right then, come and have tea with me at four o'clock, and we can talk about your affairs.' Then he left. I told Mrs Wessels I was sure he already knew exactly what my plans were. Old Thomson had no doubt told him everything in advance. Mrs Wessels, however, assured me that he wouldn't listen to others, and that I should be pleased he'd invited me for tea because, as far as she was aware, he'd never extended such an invitation to anyone else.

By four o'clock that afternoon I was there. He met me on the stoep and invited me in. When I entered I saw that a few other officers were also present, and I started feeling fearful once more. Were they trying to trap me, or were they also just there for tea? I summoned up all my good manners, and tried to behave as best I could. We talked away merrily, and whenever the conversation turned to the battlefield, I laughed and gave an evasive answer.

When it was time for me to leave, I asked him if it would be possible for me to go to my parents, provided of course that Commandant Thomson could find out where they were. He looked me straight in the eye and said, 'If you pay your own travel expenses.'

My heart pounded! They must know about the money I had on me, and now they were trying to trap me. I had to be very careful now. So I shrugged my shoulders and said, 'Where will I get the money from? How is it that you can afford to transport everyone else but not me?'

'Your case is different,' the old man answered. 'You are in one camp and want to move to another of your own accord. It is not we who are sending you there, so you must pay for the ticket yourself. I will inform Commandant Thomson of your request.' I turned to walk away, but he called me back and gave me a beautiful bunch of flowers. I accepted it and thanked him. He asked me if I'd walked from the camp, and when I replied that I had he offered to give me a lift back as he was going to the camp on business. He dropped me at the gate, and went off to Commandant Thomson's tent. What they said to each other I'll never know, but Thomson later sent for me and told me he'd written to Bethulie, and would let me know when he received word from them.

NINE

After receiving this promise from the Commandant I felt entirely satisfied with life, for I could now live each day with the hope of news of my parents. At long last I would discover whether they were alive, and even if I couldn't go to them, at least I would know whether I'd be able to see them when the war was over. And I felt sure the war wouldn't last too much longer. There was absolutely nothing to do in the camp—every day was exactly the same. On Sundays there was at least church to go to, although it was also very sad as some of the people had lost their faith. Others said they had to fetch and cook food, and that now was no time for religion—they had to fight just to keep body and soul together.

One Monday the women were really annoyed. There was no firewood. The Khaki-Boers had been out looking for wood the previous day, and the Afrikaners had captured them, taken their mules, given them a good hiding, 'shaken them out', and chased them all the way back to the camp. I didn't in the least mind going hungry that day—in fact it was one of my happiest days in the camp. I had a good laugh.

All the women went to Commandant Thomson and demanded wood. Their children were hungry. When he told them they should ask the Boers for wood, the women stormed the tent, and old Thomson fled as fast as his feet could carry him. I didn't take part in the protest, being on my best behaviour because I wanted to join my parents. When they couldn't get to the Commandant, the women picked up their axes and hammers and headed straight for a couple of Khaki-Boers who were bringing a supply of water on wagons. Before they knew what hit them, the Khaki-Boers had been chased from the wagons, the mules had been unhitched, and splinters were flying in all directions. Not long afterwards, there was a pot of food cooking at every tent! I was amazed that despite all the hardship and sadness, these women had not lost their spirit as Afrikaners.

One afternoon I was sitting talking to a friend in my tent when the Commandant walked in and announced that he wished to see me in his office at four o'clock. I had no idea what to expect, but when I arrived at his office that afternoon he was very friendly and said, 'Look, I wrote to the camp at Bethulie. Your parents are there, but people are being sent from there to Uitenhage. If your parents go to Uitenhage, I'll grant your request. I'll probably know within a few days.' Then he added, 'You mustn't go to Bethulie. You're better off here. You'd probably never get out of there alive.'

I thought then that he was only saying that because he didn't want to send me to my parents, but I later discovered just how bad things really were at Bethulie. I was about to leave when I remembered the problem of my travel expenses, and I asked, 'But what about my travel expenses?'

'Oh,' he replied, 'those you will have to pay yourself.'

'But how can you ask that of me? Where will I get the money? I will have to work first and earn some money.' He shrugged his shoulders in reply. I asked him how much it would cost and he told me £5. 'Well,' I said, 'then I will never get away from here. Where will I get £5 from?'

Again I was in difficulty. I could use some of the money I'd taken from my father, but how would I explain it to the enemy?

Where would I tell them the money had come from? It seemed to me that they must know I had money, so once again I lay awake at night making plans. I had for so long carried the money next to my heart, day and night—would they now catch me like this? No, I would make another plan. I would go to Mrs van Wyk, a good friend, luckily also well off, and tell her that I wanted to go to my parents but didn't have the money to do so. I felt very bad at the thought of being untruthful, but I decided it would be better that way. I was so shy about asking that I kept postponing the matter. Eventually I could put it off no longer. I approached her, saying, 'Mrs van Wyk, please would you lend me £5—that is, if you can trust me? I will return the money to you as soon as I reach my parents.'

'Of course I will, my child, gladly. When would you like the money?' she replied. I told her I would need it as soon as I heard where my parents were, and that I could never thank her sufficiently for helping me out of my predicament.

That evening I again lay in my tent making plans. The camp seemed to be buzzing with activity—youngsters were playing outside, and their singing filled the evening air: '*Vanaand gaan die volkies koring sny*.' I suspect the camp sounded busy because I felt so happy and satisfied. Indeed, the truth was that the youngsters had nothing to do, except play cards or *klip-klip*.

Two days passed like this until Commandant Thomson called me and told me he'd received word that my parents had been sent to Uitenhage. He asked me my father's full names, and I replied, 'Ockert Jacobus Raal.' He told me those were the names he'd been given, so it must be my father. He said further that if I'd managed to get the money together for my ticket, I could go to Kroonstad and inquire there about my departure.

'Have you got the money?' he asked.

'Oh yes,' I replied.

'And where did you get it?' he wanted to know. 'You obviously didn't earn it.'

I felt the blood rush to my face, and were it not for the fact that I longed so bitterly to be with my parents, I would've given him an angry reply. Instead I merely said, 'A friend lent me the money.'

Then he gave me a letter to give to the Commandant in Kroonstad, and I left for town the very same afternoon. There the Commandant told me that if I had the money, I could leave the next day at three o'clock, and that if I gave him the money he would give me a pass.

I quickly went and said goodbye to the few friends I had in town, then I returned to the camp. I was excited and in a hurry. In no time at all I organised and packed my things. I couldn't bear to spend even one hour alone in my tent once everything was packed, so I went from tent to tent, but still the time dragged slowly by. I felt as happy to be leaving the camp as I'd felt miserable the first day I arrived. I said goodbye to all my friends and acquaintances, and even went to the hospital to say goodbye to the nurses. I spent the last evening with Mrs Wessels, and stayed with her until it was time for lights out. Only then did I return to my tent. I still had to carry out the plan I'd come up with in connection with Mrs van Wyk's money. I was not allowed to use a lamp, but I needed light to write by, so I did what I always did when I wanted to read late at night. I sat on the ground, set the lantern down in front of me, put a thick blanket over myself and the lantern, then lit the lantern. That way the guards couldn't see the light.

Once the lantern was burning nicely, I got out my writing paper, removed the money from my chest, took out £5, and worked the tarpaulin envelope closed again. Then I placed the money Mrs van Wyk had given me in an envelope, and wrote her the following note:

'My dear Friend

A thousand times thank you for your wonderful generosity.
Behind it lie the love and trust you have given me. But I
cannot take the money. I will write and tell you why as
soon as I reach my parents. Please do not tell anyone about
this until you receive a letter from me. I know I can trust
you.
Again thank you very, very much.

Your grateful and true

Friend'

After putting the note and the money into an envelope, I put
out the light and went to bed. But sleep was not for me that night.
I was wide awake, and the thought that I was going to my parents
was enough to keep me out of bed altogether. I wondered what
my parents looked like now, whether they'd aged from all the
sadness and worry. I wondered whether they knew where my
brothers were, the brothers I'd last seen shackled together. I
wondered how long the journey to Uitenhage would take. I didn't
sleep a wink, and at the first glimmer of light I was out and about,
wandering between the tents. As soon as I saw that Mrs Wessels
and her family were up, I went directly there. She had a daughter
by the name of Christina, and we were good friends. She'd been
like a sister to me during my time in the camp. On many
occasions she came into my tent saying, 'Come on, let's play
klip-klip.' Then we would close the tent door and the two of us
would sit and play until late in the day. Some days when she
arrived I was out, and she would then usually leave me a note
addressed to:

'Miss S Raal Esq
Tent Alone, No 0
Joiner Section 4
Captured murderer and rabble-rouser
Kroonstad OFS'

I lingered awhile in Mrs Wessels' tent before bidding them farewell. Mrs Wessels said to me: 'Oh, my child, you wouldn't believe how deeply we feel about being parted from you. Only the thought that you're going to your parents comforts me.' I cried when I said goodbye to them, but they must have been tears of joy at the thought of meeting my parents, whom I'd last seen two years before in such terrible circumstances.

Then I went to the Commandant to get my pass. I wondered whether I should greet him. The 'Bird Cage' remained in my thoughts. When I entered his office, he rose and said I must wait awhile—the cart would take me to the station. Then he gave me my pass. I looked him straight in the eye, and said, 'Good day, Commandant', but did not offer my hand. He came up to me, and took my hand in his with the words, 'Good day, Miss Raal. I wish you a pleasant journey, and I hope things work out well for you.'

My first reaction was to thank him, but the feelings of hate I had for his nation overcame me once more, and like somebody with no upbringing at all I rudely turned and walked away. Even though I was very rude to him, I was at least true to myself, for it would have been dishonest of me to thank him.

Then I went to Mrs van Wyk's tent. When I said goodbye to her I gave her the note I'd written the previous evening, and said, 'Mrs van Wyk, there is something valuable in this envelope, but promise me you won't open it until tomorrow morning.'

'Certainly, I promise,' she said.

With that I was off to Kroonstad to give the Commandant there my money, and to get my ticket for the train. When I arrived

I had to wait for him until half-past two, and he then informed me that passenger trains didn't travel in the evenings, also that they would be sending someone along to help me. 'Oh, another guard?' I asked.

'No,' he replied, 'just someone to help you. The journey will take four days in all.'

Of course I knew that the 'somebody to help me' was nothing but a guard. However, I kept my own counsel.

As before the guard was dressed in khaki, but he didn't look like a regular Tommy. The look on his face was too idiotic even for that of a Tommy, and the fact that I would have to gaze at his face for the next four days seemed just too much for me!

I said goodbye to the Commandant, and he said he hoped to see me again before leaving South Africa. My guard and I then travelled to the station on the cart. The train steamed in as soon as we arrived, and in a short while we were on our way.

The first night we slept over in Bloemfontein, on the train of course. We'd brought no provisions with us, so I waited to see what my guard intended to do about food. To me he looked too much of a dolt even to get hungry, for he simply sat as if nailed to the bench opposite me. After a while I asked him about food, and he actually spoke, 'I don't know.' So I stood up and walked across to the dinning room at the station, sat down, and ordered some food. I'd barely done so when my guard arrived. When I finished eating and stood up to leave, the waiter protested that I hadn't yet paid. I gave him an indignant look, pointed to my guard, and said, 'He will pay.' And I returned to my compartment. To this day I've no idea what happened about payment, but no sooner was I back in my compartment than the guard was back as well.

When all became quiet at the station, I went and sat at an angle in one of the corners of my compartment. I wanted to get some sleep. I was truly not afraid of this Englishman—he looked too weak and tired even to draw breath. When next I looked, he lay stretched out on his bench and was soon asleep. I also slept reasonably well that night. Early next morning the station was a hive of activity, and to my great joy a woman got into our compartment with her two children. She was on her way to Zwartkop, so my time on the train would therefore not be too lonely and boring.

The next night we slept at Naauwpoort. I expected us to get to Port Elizabeth the following day, and anticipated that from there I would be able to travel to the camp. I simply couldn't wait for the time to pass. My heart was bursting with excitement.

*   *   *

We arrived at Uitenhage at nine o'clock that evening. It was pitch dark and I didn't know the place at all. I asked the guard what I should do, but as usual his reply was, 'I don't know.' I could expect nothing from him, so I decided to look for some form of transport for myself.

Being war time, however, I couldn't find anyone or anything to take me to the camp, so I deposited my luggage in the waiting room and, after obtaining a receipt, began making accommodation plans for the night. I couldn't walk to the camp as it was three miles outside town and, besides, I had no idea in which direction. I began looking for an hotel, and of course my guard tagged along wherever I went.

Reaching a guest house of sorts, I told the guard to wait for me on the stoep, walked into the house, and encountered a woman in the passage. I asked her if I could spend the night, but she answered that the house was full. However, she gave me the address of two German women who took in lodgers, and I left. The Englishman was still on the stoep, but I ignored him. I headed for the German ladies' house, trailed of course by my guard. I knocked on the door, and one of the ladies answered it herself. I asked her in Afrikaans whether she had a room for me for the night. She asked whether I was alone, for she'd noticed the Englishman behind me. I stood closer and quickly explained to her who he was. I told her I had nothing to do with him, and that I'd explain everything once he'd gone. I wasn't afraid to speak to her openly because I knew what the Germans had done for us in the concentration camps. She invited me in, and I told the Englishman he would have to find his own place for the night, and that he could meet me there the following afternoon, but not before four o'clock as I wanted to rest. Suddenly he woke up and asked the lady if she had a place for him as well, but she told him the house was full. We walked in and closed the door behind us.

That evening I enjoyed a wonderful dinner, and I told them everything—who I was, the circumstances in which I found myself, life on commando—and they told me about the camp outside town. We talked late into the night.

Again I couldn't fall asleep that night. A hundred and one thoughts kept me awake. I was afraid the guard might report me—I'd treated him so badly—and that I might be recaptured. They'd never believe me if I told them how useless he'd been, and I wanted to have a plan to ensure that I would at least see my parents before they could lock me up again.

Next morning I asked the two ladies for advice, and they told me they had a horse and cart with which they could send me to the camp. I had only to collect my things from the station, but I was too afraid to go there. If I went, I might immediately be recaptured. They told me I should give my luggage receipt to their younger brother, and he would do the necessary at nine o'clock when the station opened.

At nine o'clock he went to the station and we got everything ready, so that when he returned we could immediately leave for the camp. If I were recaptured after that, I would at least have been able to see my parents, and life in prison wouldn't then seem so bad. Not much after nine the boy returned with my things. I said goodbye to my friends, and asked how much all their kindness cost, but they wouldn't accept a thing.

When we approached the camp, the boy said he couldn't enter as he didn't have permission to do so. I told him, 'Don't say that, you must take me in. *They* sent me here, and now I have to get in. Drive straight to the Commandant's house so I can tell him I'm here.' We stopped in front of his house and the Commandant came outside. The boy climbed down from the cart, but I remained seated. He asked the boy who was in the cart, and the boy mentioned my name.

He walked briskly up to the cart and said, 'Who gave you the right to come here without a guard?'

'I did,' I replied.

'Where is your guard?' he wanted to know.

'I've no idea. It's not my job to look after him, it's his job to look after me. I wasn't going to sit around in town running up costs. I was sent to my parents at this camp. That's why I'm here.'

Then I added, 'You must pay this boy for my lodging. It is £1 for the cart and for my lodging. The Commandant at Kroonstad said you had to take care of me.'

I could see that the Commandant was very angry, but he actually took out the money and gave it to the boy. Then I asked him where my parents were, and he gave me the number of their hut. The boy and I walked away, and when we were out of earshot he asked me if his sisters had really charged that much for one night's lodging. 'No, they charged me nothing,' I replied, 'but the old Commandant was far too cheeky, so I made him pay for it.'

TEN

The number of my parents' hut was twenty one. The closer we got, the more my heart pounded. By the time we got to number eighteen, it felt as if my heart had already reached number twenty one, and only my body was still walking. When we stopped in front of number twenty one, my father was standing in the doorway of the hut. Of course they knew nothing of my arrival.

I couldn't believe my eyes when I saw him, he was so emaciated. I sat on the cart like a dumb person. My father looked at me, shouted to my mother and the others, and they all rushed out to greet me. They almost pulled me from the cart. I couldn't speak. 'My child, are you not pleased to see us?' asked my father.

I replied, '*Ag*, father, how could you even think such a thing? I'm just so upset because you all look so wasted. I hardly recognise you.'

My mother, who couldn't stop crying, continued along similar lines, 'How can you say that, my child? Have you not also been in a camp?'

'Yes, mother, but you look as if you could die at any moment. It doesn't look as if any of you will ever leave this camp alive.'

'That is from hunger,' my mother replied. 'The camp at Bethulie almost did us in. We *all* almost died there.'

When we calmed down and could talk normally, my mother wanted to know where my brothers were, and what condition

112

they'd been in when I last saw them. I had to protect her from the worst. Why should I cause further pain to her already broken body and heart? If I told her the truth, it would probably kill her. I thought of the last time I'd seen them. Jacobus in a pair of jodhpurs that were far too small for him, bare legs, two *veldskoens* that had only a small strip of leather across the toes and nothing behind the heel. There were holes in the soles of the shoes through which *riempies* were threaded and tied around the leg. He had no shirt, just a tattered jacket to protect him from the cold, sun and wind. Abram did not even have a jacket, only a shirt without sleeves. The sleeves had been used to patch the shirt. He also wore a patched pair of khaki trousers, and two makeshift shoes. He had no hat, only a sort of knitted woollen cap. How could I ever tell my mother all this? So I simply asked her whether she knew where my brothers were. She told me she'd heard they were in India. She'd written to make sure, and was waiting for a reply.

By now I could contain myself no longer. I walked over to my old father, put my arms around his neck, and said, 'Do you know, my dear father, that I still have £500 and all the receipts, including those the English gave me at Boomplaas for all the sheep and the wagons?' I removed the tarpaulin envelope from my chest and pressed it into his hands, saying, 'Father, take this. I thank the Lord that I could save it for you and mother. I'm glad to be rid of it—it's given me many bitter days and nights. It's not much, but at least it's enough with which to make a new start when we get out of here.' My father did not speak. He simply hugged me close to his heart, which gave me greater pleasure than any words he could have spoken.

Despite the fact that we were still living in a camp, I was completely happy now that I was with my parents. The Commandant was the only fly in the ointment. He couldn't stand me, and when even the smallest thing went wrong in the camp he always saw me as the cause. 'That Miss Raal is just a curse to me in this camp!' he declared.

*   *   *

One day I received a letter from a friend in the town, saying I should meet him that afternoon at the camp fence. It was the practice that one's friends were not allowed to come into the camp, but they could stand at the camp fence—on the outside, of course, with us on the inside. In this manner we could converse. That afternoon I walked nonchalantly up to the fence, but I was there for no more than two seconds when the Commandant arrived and asked me what I was doing there. I in turn asked him what all the other people were doing there. He said that that had nothing to do with it, and that I had no right to stand there and talk.

'And why not?' I wanted to know.

'Because you're a trouble maker,' he said, and he grabbed my arm and tried to drag me away from the fence. I pulled myself free, and told him I wouldn't move another step unless the others also moved. By now people were staring at us in surprise, waiting to see what would happen. My friend handed me a basket over the fence and advised me to go back. The Commandant tried to snatch the basket from my hand, but I grabbed it back and said, '*Engelsman*, try that once more and you'll never see your office again.' I was standing directly in front of him when I said this. Then I turned my back on him, lent against the fence, and started chatting to my friend.

When I turned round later, he was gone. The following day I received a letter from him saying that I was not allowed to set foot outside the camp. I paid no attention to this, and went out a great deal. One day I even went to Port Elizabeth with some friends. We missed our train, and only arrived back at the camp after ten o'clock that night. I wasn't afraid because I knew the Commandant never left his house after dark. He was too afraid of the Boers and, who knows, maybe even of me. He couldn't stand me, of that I was certain. He even went so far as to prohibit me from receiving parcels through the post. I went and told him, 'If you dare stop my things, I'll go and fetch them in Uitenhage and, not only that, I'll lay a charge against you. You've no reason to stop my post.' After that I started receiving my post once more. My parcels were usually large because I received a lot of rusks, biltong and fruit from people. Everything had to pass through his hands, and he couldn't bear it. But in spite of all this, I was happy because I was with my parents, and I hoped I'd be able to stay with them until peace was declared.

*   *   *

I shall never forget the morning of 31 May 1902 when Richards, the camp Commandant, gave us notice that we were all to appear in front of his office at nine o'clock. When we got there, he was standing on a cart to which two mules were hitched. He stood upright on the bench of the cart, and had a cypress stick in one hand. When nine o'clock came, he said only, 'There is peace, there is peace, the Boers have lost their country!' Then he jumped off the bench, sat down, spurred the mules on, and raced away.

For probably a full five minutes a deathly hush fell over us all. Then came the sound of sobbing. It seemed as if those sobs forced the truth into our collective consciousness, and only then did we fully realise what the Commandant had said. Some women were crawling around on the ground groaning, and in every hut there was crying and moaning. Others shouted aloud, 'He's lying, he's lying!' Old mothers walked with bowed heads, grieving in silence. Some tore up their Bibles, shouting, 'I don't believe in anything anymore. This defeat is too unjust!' The 'joiners' threw their hats in the air and shouted 'Hooray!' It was a sorry spectacle. I ran to our hut and buried my head in my pillow. I just wanted to be alone. I was broken-hearted. Time, only time, could heal the pain.

Our poor people, how terrible they looked: sunburnt, hungry, and wasted with anxiety and despair. And I knew what they didn't yet know—what the houses looked like to which they must return. They would have to leave the camp with virtually nothing, and what awaited them on the outside were destroyed farms, burnt-out houses, and slaughtered animals. All the trees were dead and gone, and nothing remained alive on the farms. Who could ever forget? How many men and children lay buried in the camps, wrapped in a khaki-blanket? And what future was there for the widows, what awaited them on the farms when they returned with their few young children? ...

The people in the camps were now sent in dribs and drabs to their homes which no longer existed. We wanted to take nothing with us from the camp. We wanted no reminder. Who needed a reminder of that which they could never forget?

Every family was dropped off at the station closest to their home—we arrived at Edenburg at three o'clock in the morning. Luckily my father had a house in the town, and we went directly there, each of us with a bundle on our backs. When we arrived at the house we saw it was occupied. My father and mother sat down on their bundles on the stoep, not knowing what to do. I became extremely angry. I was about to knock on the door when my father stopped me, saying we might get into trouble again. But it was our house, and who had the right to live in our house without our permission? I knocked on the window, but nobody answered. Then I knocked quite loudly on the front door. Somebody inside asked who it was, and I said, 'Come and open up!' I heard someone walking to the door. When the door opened,

I saw it was a man. He spoke bluntly, 'Why the devil are you knocking on my door in the middle of the night? Who are you?'

'I'm the owner of this house, and you'd better open up quickly,' I replied. 'My parents are exhausted, and we want to come inside.'

He said he first wanted to speak to his wife. When he returned, we were already inside the house. My father told him it was his house, and asked how it came about that he was living there. The man told him the English had said he could live there.

When his wife came out she was quite calm, and not long after that the man apologised for the manner in which he'd spoken to me.

We had to wait until three o'clock the following day for the wagon to take us to the farm. In the meanwhile my father had come to an arrangement with the man regarding the house. He would rent the house, as we wouldn't be needing it in a hurry. We had no horse left alive, nor any other animal, so how would we get to church in town anyway?

At three o'clock the wagon arrived to take us to the farm. We made things as comfortable as possible for our parents, and loaded the food we'd been given for fourteen days, which consisted of tins of salted bully beef and flour. Then we departed, with six mules pulling the wagon. It was an uncomfortable journey—we were shaken and rattled, and fell over one another. My parents had to hold on so as not to fall off the wagon, and it was a full fourteen miles to the farm. We couldn't wait to arrive. As we approached the farmhouse, I saw tears running down my dear father's cheeks. My mother turned her face so we couldn't see it, but we children were crying, laughing and shouting all at once, and the two drivers stared at us in bewilderment. No pen can describe the depths of gratitude and freedom we felt.

*   *   *

We noticed that the roof of the house was still intact. As we approached, we saw that the doors and windows had been broken out. When the wagon stopped in front of the doorway, we children flew off like sheets of paper blown by the wind, and stormed into the house. My parents were now calm and quiet. They brought in the food, and our other belongings. Then the wagon left. Food and rest were the last things on our young minds—we wanted to investigate. Of course there was no trace of our furniture, and the house was completely empty. We walked around outside. The first living thing we encountered was a wild cat, which had taken up residence with its kittens in the kitchen. We were still looking at the cat when my little brother called to us to come outside. We ran outside and what did we see? A whole troop of springbok and blesbok were grazing outside our door, as tame as could be. Nobody had bothered them during the three years we'd been away, and everything had grown wild. Almost all the big trees were dead, and there was no sign of our flower garden. The big dam was bone dry, and the earth was cracked. The water ditches were all overgrown, and wild animals had moved into the house. For us youngsters it was nothing—we were happy to be alive and free. But when I looked at my mother and father, I could see the look of hopelessness on their faces. We didn't even have a table and chairs. How they must have missed the comfortable life of old. Everything they'd sweated and worked for was destroyed and gone, and now was the time they needed it most, when they were weak and exhausted and hungry and tired. Would they ever be able to forgive and forget? Even today I cannot bear to think about it. The wounds are still too raw and too deep, and although time will heal them, the scars will always remain.

We started making plans about where to spend the night. We had to seek out the most sheltered corners of the house, as there were no windows or doors, and we were afraid that wild animals might come into the house. We also couldn't light a candle, for the house was so windy that candlelight was impossible. It was a terrible feeling that first night in the big, empty house.

We decided that my parents should sleep in the children's room. The door was gone, but there were still a few window panes for some comfort. We youngsters went to sleep in one of the other rooms. That afternoon we collected a pile of stones to throw at wild animals during the night. We were barely in our room when we heard my mother scream. We grabbed a couple of stones and ran to their room. When we entered we saw a huge wild cat sitting in the window, and the animal was so brazen that he was entirely unmoved by my father's attempts to scare him off. My father had nothing to throw, but before he could speak our stones rained down on the cat. The cat was gone in a second, but so were the few remaining window panes. Our parents then moved to the room where we were supposed to be sleeping, although the floor was so hard that we simply sat there the entire night, moaning and groaning. I was so bitter that night that I said terrible things. Each time my father had to stop me.

We were all pleased when the first night was over. The following day we collected planks and wood which my father nailed together in front of their bedroom door. That would have to do to start with. We scrounged around again on the farm. There was nothing else for us to do, or rather there was, but we didn't have the necessary tools. We had absolutely nothing, not even a pick or a shovel. Both my brothers were still in India, and we had no idea when they'd be coming home. My father was old, and he couldn't manage the ruined farm on his own. The task of helping him fell to my younger sister and me. There was nothing to do in the house—there was no food to be cooked, except porridge, and there was nothing to clean as there was nothing in the house. Our living conditions were worse than those of our farm labourers had ever been. We couldn't live on bully beef and porridge alone, and in any event we only had enough for fourteen days. We had to make a plan. The first thing we did was clean the fountain, so we could get clean water. When we returned home in the evenings I was absolutely exhausted. My sister was too tired to eat, and my father's legs could barely carry him. And after a hard day's work, we had to be satisfied with bully beef and dry bread.

We decided that one of us would walk to Kruger Station, an hour's ride by horse from our farm, catch the train from there to Edenburg, and buy food there. One couldn't buy too much, however, as it had to be carried back to the farm from the station in the afternoon. One day my father went to town and bought an old cart and two old horses, for which he had to pay quite a steep price to the Repatriation Board. But at least we could then transport things far more easily.

Later my father went by train to the Cape Colony to buy sheep with the money that had caused me so much heartache. He bought four hundred ewes, and drove them back to the farm. He managed to pick up the sheep cheaply, and he still had a good deal of money left over. In the meanwhile we employed a farm labourer, cleaned in front of the farmhouse, and soon there was water in the dam once more. We started a vegetable garden, the two horses picked up well, and by the time my father returned the place almost looked like a farm again.

When they heard in town that my father had bought sheep, they immediately cancelled our rations. Luckily we could help ourselves further.

After we'd been on the farm a few months, we heard that they were compensating people for goods taken from them or burnt— provided of course that they had receipts to prove a claim. I told my father that now was our chance, and that we should send them the receipts they had given me at Boomplaas. We did so, and a week or two later my father received a letter from the Commandant saying that as the proof was in his daughter's name, he could not lodge a claim if she were dead.

My father and I went into town to see the Commandant. He was very surprised to see me, or perhaps disappointed, for he started asking me all sorts of questions which had nothing at all to do with the payment of compensation. Among other things, he asked me whether I'd fought. I said, 'What of it?'

'You see,' he said, 'I don't know if we can actually pay out a woman. You were not supposed to fight.' He looked at me again and asked, 'Did you fight?'

'Only in self defence,' I answered. He remained silent, and looked again at the receipt. It was for £1 090. Then he asked my father if all the goods had belonged to him. My father confirmed that this was so, but added that four hundred of the sheep had belonged to my brother. Then the Commandant said he couldn't pay out for those sheep, and gave us only £900. He also didn't want to pay out for the three hundred 'Blue Backs' I'd got from Commandant Fourie for the £300 he'd taken from me. He would send that claim to Pretoria and find out what the position was. A while later he wrote to tell us that they couldn't pay out, and added that the Boer Generals should pay because they'd used the money. He added that they wouldn't return the 'Blue Backs' and were keeping them as a forfeiture.

Truly we had to make a whole new start. My two unmarried brothers, Jacobus and Abram, who were taken prisoner with me, had been sent to India. After the peace they refused to swear the oath of allegiance to the English Queen, and remained there for seventeen months, but eventually they were forced to return for health reasons. My mother missed them terribly. Then one day she told us she'd had a dream in which her sons came back to the farm. That very same day a cart arrived with my brothers on it. There is no need to describe our reunion ... They were now grown men, and immediately threw themselves into the farmwork to help the family forge ahead once more.

121

Glossary of Terms

ag, similar to the Scottish *och* or the English *oh*, often used fondly
biltong, dried strips of venison or beef
Blue-backs, Boer voucher for money or goods
braai, cook over an open fire
burgher, citizen, a reference to the Boers
droë wors, literally, dried sausage
Engelsman, Englishman
Here, the Lord
inspan, harness
ja-nee, literally, yes-no
joiner, Boer who joined and fought for the enemy
kappie, linen sun-bonnet
kêrel, chap or young man
Khaki, slang for a British soldier
Khaki-Boer, a Boer co-operating with the enemy
klap, clout
kleinbasie, young master
kleinmies, young miss or madam
kleinnooi, young miss
klip-klip, literally, 'stone-stone,' a game played with stones
konka, cooking tin
kopje, low hill
laager, Boer encampment
magtie, exclamation of surprise
nefie, young cousin or young man, not limited to relatives
nonnie, young woman, used fondly
oom, uncle, a widely used term of respect not limited to relatives
opsaal, saddle up
ou bees, literally, old animal, meaning 'old thing' or 'old chap'
riempie, strip made of hide or skin
shake out,   the act of stripping and packing off an enemy soldier without uniform, rifle, or horse
spider, a type of horse-drawn cart
toe maar, don't worry (*now then* in context on page 26)
trek oxen, oxen used for pulling wagons
Vanaand gaan die volkies koring sny, popular folk song to this day, 'Tonight the folk are going to harvest corn'
veldskoen, shoe of soft untanned leather
wragtie, exclamation of interest or surprise